Income Stability

How to Build Predictable, Durable, and Resilient Income

MARK ELLISON

PERENNIAL PUBLISHING

Published by Perennial Publishing

First Edition

Paperback ISBN: 978-971996-15-8
Hardcover ISBN: 978-971996-16-5
EBook ISBN: 978-971996-17-2

For bulk or institutional orders, contact Perennial Publishing.

Contents

Income Stability

Income is commonly understood as a number. It is presented as a level, compared across individuals, tracked over time, and used as a primary indicator of financial position. It appears in annual totals, monthly figures, and incremental increases. It is evaluated in terms of growth, decline, and relative standing. This framing is simple, measurable, and widely accepted. It allows income to be discussed, compared, and targeted with clarity.

But this framing is incomplete.

A number exists at a moment. It captures a snapshot, not a process. It implies stability where there may be none, and continuity where none is guaranteed. When income is reduced to a number, its behavior across time disappears. The conditions under which it is produced, the intervals at which it arrives, and the variability it exhibits are removed from view. What remains is a static representation of something inherently dynamic.

This is where the misunderstanding begins.

Income does not exist as a fixed level. It exists as a sequence. It arrives, pauses, fluctuates, and sometimes stops. It is distributed unevenly across time and influenced by factors that are not constant. A monthly figure may appear stable, but the underlying process that produces it may not be. A yearly total may appear sufficient, but the path taken to reach it may include periods of absence or compression. The number conceals the structure that generates it.

Time is the dimension that reveals this structure. When income is observed across time rather than at a single point, its properties become visible. It is no longer a single value but a pattern. The spacing between inflows, changes in magnitude, and interruptions all define how income behaves. These characteristics determine whether income can support the system it is meant to sustain. Without time, these characteristics remain invisible.

Variability is one of the primary features that emerges when income is viewed across time. Inflows are rarely identical in amount or timing. They expand and contract, shift forward and backward, and respond to changing conditions. This variability is not an anomaly; it is a structural property of income. Even in systems that appear stable, variation exists beneath the surface. The appearance of consistency often reflects a limited view rather than an absence of change.

Interruption is another inherent condition. There are periods in which inflow is reduced, delayed, or absent. These interruptions may be brief or extended, visible or subtle. They may occur suddenly or develop gradually. Regardless of form, they introduce discontinuity into the flow of income. When income is treated as a number, these interruptions are averaged out or ignored. When it is treated as a sequence, they become central to understanding system behavior.

The presence of variability and interruption changes the question entirely. The issue is no longer how much income exists at a given moment, but whether the system can continue to function as income fluctuates or stops. Stability cannot be defined by the absence of change, because change is constant. It must be defined by the system's ability to operate through that change.

This shifts the focus from level to structure.

Income does not operate in isolation. It interacts with a set of obligations that persist across time. These obligations require continuity. They occur at specific intervals, demand specific amounts, and do not adjust automatically in response to income conditions. The system must therefore reconcile a variable inflow with a structured outflow. This interaction creates tension between how income behaves and what it is required to support.

This tension is not resolved by increasing income alone. A higher number does not eliminate variability, nor does it guarantee continuity. If income arrives irregularly or is interrupted, the system must still bridge those gaps. If obligations are fixed and inflow is not, the system must absorb the difference. The problem is not simply one of magnitude, but of compatibility. The structure of income must align with the structure of what it supports.

This is why stability is often misdefined.

Stability is frequently associated with high income or consistent pay. These conditions can contribute to stability, but they do not define it. A system may have high income and still experience instability if that income is irregular or dependent on conditions that can change. A system may appear consistent yet still contain underlying fragility if its continuity depends on assumptions that are not guaranteed. Stability cannot be inferred from appearance alone. It must be evaluated based on how the system behaves across time.

The source of this behavior is structural rather than behavioral.

Outcomes are often attributed to discipline, effort, or decision-making. These factors matter, but they operate within structural constraints. The structure of income—how it is generated, how it varies, and how it interacts with obligations—defines the conditions under which decisions are made. When instability occurs, it is often the result of structural mismatch rather than individual failure. The system produces outcomes consistent with its design.

Understanding income as a system requires a different perspective.

Instead of viewing income as a number to be increased, it must be viewed as a flow to be understood. This flow moves across time, shaped by variability and interruption, constrained by external conditions, and required to support continuous obligations. The system must convert this flow into sustained function, absorbing deviations and maintaining continuity. The question becomes not how much income exists, but how it behaves and whether that behavior is compatible with the system it supports.

Constraint is an inherent part of this system.

Income does not operate in unlimited space. It is subject to limits in timing, capacity, and conditions. Adjustments cannot be made instantly or without cost. The system cannot be continuously reconfigured to match ideal conditions. It must operate within what is possible at any given moment. These constraints define how the system responds to variability and interruption, shaping its ability to maintain continuity.

Within this constrained environment, the system must manage the tension between inflow and obligation. It must absorb variability, bridge interruptions, and sustain function across time. The effectiveness of this process depends on how the system is structured. Some structures allow for adjustment and persistence, while others amplify disruption and lead to breakdown. The difference lies not in the amount of income, but in how it is organized and how it behaves.

This leads to a different formulation of the core question.

If income is not a number, and stability is not defined by level, then what determines whether a system remains stable? The answer lies in how income behaves across time and how that behavior interacts with the system's requirements. Stability emerges when the system can continue to function despite variability, interruption, and constraint. It is not a condition of perfection, but of persistence.

This book is concerned with that persistence.

It does not focus on increasing income, optimizing earnings, or prescribing specific actions. It does not offer strategies for maximizing returns or reducing expenses. Its purpose is to examine how income behaves as a system, how that system responds to real-world conditions, and what determines whether it remains functional across time. The emphasis is on structure, not tactics; on behavior, not outcomes.

To engage with this perspective requires a shift in how income is observed.

The focus must move from static measures to dynamic behavior. Instead of asking what income is at a point in time, the question becomes how it moves, how it changes, and how it interacts with the system it supports. Patterns, timing, and continuity become central. The system must be viewed as a sequence of events rather than a single value.

This shift alters how stability is understood.

Stability is no longer the absence of fluctuation or the presence of a high number. It becomes the system's ability to sustain its function across time despite variability and interruption. It is defined by continuity rather than consistency, by persistence rather than level. The system is stable when it continues to operate, not when it appears unchanged.

This perspective does not simplify income. It makes it more accurate.

By recognizing income as a flow across time, the underlying structure becomes visible. Variability and interruption are no longer hidden within averages. Constraints are acknowledged rather than ignored. The interaction between inflow and obligation is examined in terms of compatibility rather than magnitude. The system can then be understood in terms of how it behaves rather than how it appears.

What follows builds on this foundation.

Income will be examined as a process that unfolds across time, influenced by variability, shaped by structure, and constrained by real conditions. The focus will remain on how the system operates, how it responds to disruption, and what determines its ability to continue. The objective is not to change income, but to understand it in its correct form.

Income is not a number. It is a flow across time under constraint.

This distinction is not conceptual. It determines how the system is understood and how its behavior is interpreted. When income is treated as a number, instability appears unexpected and difficult to explain. When it is understood as a flow, variability and interruption become inherent, and the question shifts from why disruption occurs to whether the system can continue through it.

The analysis that follows proceeds from this perspective. Income will not be evaluated as a level to be increased, but as a process to be examined. Its movement across time, its interaction with constraint, and its ability to sustain function will define the system. What matters is not what income is at any moment, but whether it continues in a way the system can absorb.

Stability begins with this recognition.

Income Is Not a Number

Income is often understood as a fixed figure assigned to a period of time. It is referenced as a salary, a monthly total, or an annual amount, and treated as a stable attribute of a financial system. This representation allows income to be compared, categorized, and evaluated without reference to how it is generated or how it arrives. The number becomes the point of focus, and the process that produces it recedes from view.

The distinction between a point-in-time representation and a time-based flow determines whether the structure of income is visible. A snapshot compresses multiple periods into a single value, presenting income as though it exists independently of variation and interruption. A time-based representation preserves the sequence of inflows, showing how income enters the system across successive intervals. When income is understood as a flow, it becomes clear that the system is supported not by a number, but by the pattern through which income arrives and persists.

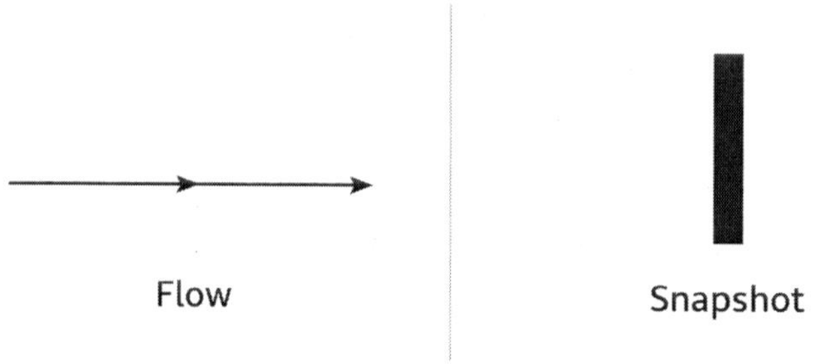

Figure 1– Flow vs Snapshot

The persistence of the numerical framing is rooted in its convenience. A single value simplifies comparison, enables aggregation, and allows income to be categorized without reference to its underlying behavior. This simplification is reinforced by reporting structures that summarize income over standardized periods, such as monthly or annual intervals. These summaries are not designed to capture variability or timing; they are designed to produce a stable representation that can be easily communicated and compared. The numerical form therefore becomes the default lens through which income is interpreted, even though it excludes the factors that determine how income interacts with the financial system.

Once income is reduced to a number, the mechanisms that shape its behavior are no longer visible. Variability within the period is absorbed into the total, and the sequence of inflows is replaced by assumed continuity. This creates the appearance of stability. Fluctuations within the period are averaged, and irregular timing is treated as though it were evenly distributed. The resulting figure suggests that income arrives in a smooth and predictable manner, even when the underlying flow is uneven or discontinuous. The stability that appears in the snapshot is therefore a function of aggregation, not a property of the flow itself.

This aggregation effect introduces a structural distinction between reported income and experienced income. Reported income reflects the total assigned to a period after variability has been compressed into a single value. Experienced income reflects the actual sequence of inflows as they occur, including their timing, spacing, and variation in magnitude. These two representations can diverge significantly even when they produce the same total. A system that receives income at irregular intervals may report the same amount as a system with consistent inflows, yet the experienced conditions within those systems differ. The timing of inflows determines when resources are available relative to obligations, and this timing cannot be inferred from the aggregated total.

The usability of income is governed by its temporal alignment with the system's outflows. Obligations within a household structure do not occur as a single event; they are distributed across time, often with fixed intervals and defined due dates. Income must intersect with these obligations at specific points. When inflows are consistent and aligned with these intervals, the system maintains continuity without requiring adjustment. When inflows are delayed or irregular, the system enters periods in which obligations persist without corresponding replenishment. These periods are not visible in the reported number, but they define the system's operational state.

Averages play a central role in maintaining the illusion of stability. By definition, an average smooths variation across periods, producing a central value that represents the total divided by time. This smoothing conceals both the magnitude and timing of deviations. Large inflows can offset periods of low or absent income within the average, creating a representation that appears stable even when the flow is uneven. The average therefore functions as a masking mechanism, removing the visibility of variability while preserving the total. The resulting figure implies continuity that may not exist in the underlying sequence.

The effect of this masking becomes more pronounced as variability increases. In a system with high variability, the difference between periods can be substantial, yet the average remains unchanged. This creates a condition in which reported income suggests stability while experienced income reflects fluctuation. The system must then absorb these fluctuations through other means, as the timing of inflows no longer aligns with the timing of obligations. The reliance on averages obscures this requirement, since the variability that necessitates adjustment is not visible in the aggregated figure.

Over time, the behavior of income reveals patterns that are not captured in snapshot representations. A flow that appears stable in aggregate may exhibit cycles, irregular intervals, or intermittent disruptions when observed over time. These patterns determine whether the system can maintain continuity without structural strain. A consistent pattern of inflows, even at a lower magnitude, can support stability if it aligns with the timing of obligations. An inconsistent pattern, even at a higher aggregate level, can introduce repeated periods of misalignment that require adjustment. Stability is therefore a function of pattern, not magnitude.

The distinction between short-term and long-term behavior further illustrates the limitations of the numerical framing. In the short term, variability may appear as isolated deviations that do not significantly alter the aggregate. In the long term, these deviations accumulate, revealing whether the flow is governed by a stable pattern or by irregular fluctuations. A system that appears stable in a single period may exhibit instability across multiple periods as the sequence of inflows reveals inconsistency. The numerical representation cannot capture this accumulation, as it resets observation at each reporting interval.

Across extended time horizons, the compression introduced by numerical representation produces an additional distortion. When income is evaluated over longer sequences, aggregating multiple periods into a single figure removes not only variability within each period, but also the relationships between periods. The order in which inflows occur, the spacing between them, and the consistency of their intervals form a structure that unfolds across time. When these elements are collapsed into an aggregate, the continuity of the sequence is replaced by implied uniformity that does not exist in the underlying flow. The system is then interpreted as though each period contributes evenly to the total, even when the sequence is irregular.

As this compression persists across successive reporting intervals, small deviations within individual periods accumulate into structural patterns that remain unobserved in the numerical form. Delays, clustering of inflows, and variation in magnitude begin to form sequences that either reinforce or weaken continuity. These sequences determine whether income behaves as a stable input or as a series of intermittent events. Because the numerical representation resets observation at each interval, these sequences are not preserved. The system is therefore evaluated as a series of independent periods rather than as a continuous process defined by relationships between periods.

Time exposes both visible and hidden variability. Visible variability appears as fluctuations large enough to affect the aggregate within a period. Hidden variability occurs within the period and is absorbed into the average, leaving the reported figure unchanged. Both forms influence system behavior, but only the former is partially reflected in the snapshot. The latter remains concealed, even though it may affect the timing of inflows relative to obligations. The presence of hidden variability means that stable reported income can coexist with unstable experienced conditions.

As income unfolds across time, the sequence of inflows determines how the system responds to disruption. A flow with consistent timing and low variability can absorb minor disruptions without altering its structure. A flow with irregular timing or high variability may experience amplification, where disruptions extend intervals between inflows or reduce their magnitude in ways that compound existing instability. These responses are path-dependent, meaning the effect of a disruption depends on the sequence that precedes it. The numerical representation, which treats each period independently, cannot account for this dependency.

Failure emerges when income is interpreted as a static number rather than a time-based process. When the system is evaluated based on reported income alone, the variability and timing embedded in the flow are excluded from analysis. This exclusion leads to a misreading of continuity, where a stable number is taken as evidence of a stable flow. The system is then structured under the assumption that inflows will occur consistently, even when the underlying sequence does not support that assumption. The result is a structural mismatch between expected and actual conditions.

This mismatch produces planning errors rooted in misinterpretation of timing. When income is assumed to be evenly distributed, obligations are positioned without regard to the actual arrival of inflows. This creates intervals in which obligations must be met in the absence of income, introducing compression within the system. These intervals may be brief or extended, depending on flow variability, but they are not visible in the numerical representation. The system therefore encounters periods of strain that were not anticipated, because the timing of inflows was not incorporated into its structure.

When this misinterpretation persists, timing mismatches begin to form a progression rather than a series of isolated events. An initial misalignment between inflow and obligation may be absorbed without immediate consequence. However, as subsequent inflows follow the same irregular pattern, the intervals between replenishment and obligation begin to extend. Each instance of misalignment increases the system's dependence on the timing of the next inflow, creating a condition in which continuity is contingent rather than assured. The system shifts from operating within stable intervals to operating within gaps that must be bridged.

As these gaps become more frequent or pronounced, the system transitions from temporary strain to structural instability. The timing of inflows no longer supports the recurring structure of obligations, and the system must repeatedly compensate for the absence of alignment. This compensation is not visible in reported income, as the aggregate remains unchanged, but it defines the system's operational state. The flow is no longer continuous in its effect, even if it remains continuous in total. The failure is therefore not a reduction in income, but a breakdown in the sequence through which income sustains the system across time.

False stability arises from the persistence of the reported number across periods. As long as the aggregate remains consistent, the system appears unchanged, even if the underlying flow is shifting. Variability may increase, intervals may lengthen, or continuity may weaken, but these changes can occur without affecting the reported total. The system then operates under the assumption of stability while its underlying conditions deteriorate. This divergence between appearance and structure delays recognition of instability, allowing it to accumulate over time.

The accumulation of these conditions leads to exposure to timing gaps. A timing gap occurs when the interval between inflows exceeds the interval between obligations, creating a period in which the system must function without replenishment. These gaps are not reflected in the reported number, as they are absorbed into the aggregate. However, their presence defines the system's operational state. Repeated timing gaps indicate a breakdown in continuity, where the flow no longer supports the system's timing requirements. The severity of this breakdown depends on the length and frequency of the gaps, as well as the variability of subsequent inflows.

As these failures accumulate, the system transitions from isolated instances of misalignment to a persistent condition of instability. This transition is gradual, as each instance of misalignment may be absorbed without immediate consequence. Over time, however, the sequence of inflows reveals a pattern in which continuity is no longer maintained. The system must then operate under conditions where the timing of income is insufficient to sustain its structure. This condition is not triggered by a change in the aggregate amount of income, but by the degradation of its temporal behavior.

Income therefore functions as a time-based input whose stability is determined by variability, predictability, and continuity. Variability defines the extent to which inflows differ between periods, both in magnitude and timing. Predictability reflects the degree to which future inflows can be anticipated based on past patterns. Continuity represents the persistence of the flow without interruption. These dimensions are not properties of a number; they are properties of a sequence. They emerge only when income is observed across time, where the structure of the flow becomes visible.

The relationship between these dimensions establishes the conditions under which stability can be evaluated. High variability reduces predictability, as future inflows become less certain in both timing and magnitude. Reduced predictability weakens continuity, as interruptions and irregular intervals become more likely. Continuity, in turn, determines whether the system can maintain alignment between inflows and outflows across time. The progression from variability to predictability to continuity defines the pathway through which income influences stability. This pathway cannot be captured in a single value, as it depends on the interaction of these dimensions across multiple periods.

When income is treated as a flow, analysis shifts from magnitude to behavior. The focus moves from how much income is reported to how it arrives, how it varies, and how it persists. This shift reveals that stability is not derived from the size of income at a point in time, but from the structure of its movement through time. A system with lower reported income may exhibit higher stability if its flow is consistent and predictable. A system with higher reported income may exhibit lower stability if its flow is irregular and discontinuous. The numerical representation does not capture this distinction, as it does not preserve the temporal characteristics that define it.

The reframing of income as a time-based system establishes the basis for evaluating its role within the financial structure. It clarifies that income must be analyzed as a sequence of events, not as a static attribute. It shows that variability, predictability, and continuity are the dimensions through which income influences stability. It demonstrates that averages and aggregates conceal the conditions that determine how income behaves. By restoring temporal structure to the analysis, the system can be understood in terms of how it operates across time, rather than how it appears at a single point.

Within this framework, income is no longer interpreted as a number that represents capacity. It is understood as a process that must be observed across periods to reveal its structure. The sequence of inflows, the intervals between them, and the variability within them define the system's ability to maintain continuity. Stability is therefore a function of time-based behavior, not of static measurement. The numerical representation remains as a summary, but it no longer defines the system. The system is defined by the flow.

Income vs Cash Flow

Income, as established, functions as a flow that unfolds across time, but the existence of that flow does not imply immediate usability within a household financial system. A distinction emerges between value that has been earned and value that can be deployed. Income represents the accumulation of earned value within a defined period, while cash flow represents the portion of that value that is accessible at a given moment. These are not equivalent states. The difference between them is defined by timing and access, and that difference determines whether the system can operate continuously.

When income is earned, it enters a transitional state before it becomes usable. This transition introduces a separation between recognition and availability. A household may generate income through labor, contracts, or other productive activity, but the value created does not immediately convert into accessible resources. The delay between earning and access forms a structural boundary within the system. Income exists on one side of this boundary as earned value, while cash flow exists on the other as usable value. The system can operate only on what is accessible, not on what has been earned but remains unavailable.

This separation is embedded in the mechanisms through which income is delivered. Compensation structures, invoicing cycles, and settlement processes all introduce delays between the point at which income is generated and the point at which it becomes accessible. These delays are not incidental. They are structural features of how income flows through economic systems. A pay cycle defines when earned wages are disbursed. An invoicing process defines when completed work is converted into receivable value and when that receivable is settled. Settlement timing defines how long transactions take to clear and become available for use. Each of these mechanisms introduces a temporal gap that separates earning from access.

The presence of this gap means that income must be understood as a two-stage process. The first stage is generation, where value is created and recognized. The second stage is conversion, where that value becomes accessible within the household structure. The duration between these stages determines how long the system must operate without access to newly earned income. During this interval, the system relies on previously available resources to maintain continuity. The longer the delay, the greater the reliance on prior availability.

Figure 2 – Income vs Cash Flow Timing

The delay between earning and access introduces a temporal misalignment between inflows and obligations. Obligations within a household financial system occur according to fixed or semi-fixed schedules. They require resources at specific points in time. When income is earned but not yet accessible, it cannot be used to meet these obligations. The system must therefore bridge the interval between earning and access using existing resources. If the delay is short and consistent, this bridging requirement remains stable. If the delay is extended or variable, the requirement becomes unpredictable, introducing structural strain.

Over time, the behavior of these delays determines how income translates into usable flow. A system with consistent delays exhibits a predictable pattern of conversion from earned income to accessible cash flow. The timing of access becomes an extension of the income pattern, allowing the system to anticipate when resources will be available. In contrast, a system with variable delays introduces uncertainty into the timing of access. Even if income is generated consistently, the conversion into usable resources may fluctuate, creating periods in which access is reduced or deferred. The variability of delays therefore becomes a secondary layer of variability, distinct from the variability of income generation itself.

As these delays accumulate across periods, they shape the structure of the system's cash flow. A short delay may appear negligible within a single period, but repeated delays extend the distance between generation and access. This extension creates a persistent gap that must be managed across time. When delays are consistent, the system can maintain a stable offset between earning and access. When delays vary, the offset shifts, creating periods in which access lags further behind generation. These shifting gaps introduce discontinuities in cash flow, even when income generation remains unchanged.

The distinction between short and extended delays highlights the sensitivity of the system to timing. A short delay maintains proximity between earning and access, allowing the system to operate with minimal bridging. An extended delay increases the duration of separation, requiring the system to sustain operations without access to newly earned income. The effect of this extension is not linear. As the delay increases, the system must allocate a greater portion of its existing resources to maintain continuity, reducing its capacity to absorb additional variability. The delay therefore amplifies the impact of any disruption in income generation or access timing.

Consistency of access is as critical as the length of the delay. A system with a fixed delay can establish a stable pattern of conversion, even if the delay is relatively long. The predictability of access allows the system to align its operations with the timing of availability. A system with inconsistent delays lacks this alignment. The timing of access shifts between periods, creating uncertainty about when resources will become available. This uncertainty disrupts the system's ability to maintain continuity, as obligations may arise before access is restored. The interaction between delay length and delay consistency defines the stability of cash flow.

Failure emerges when income is assumed to be immediately usable. When the distinction between earning and access is ignored, the system is structured under the assumption that income can be deployed as soon as it is generated. This assumption removes the delay from consideration, eliminating the need to account for the interval between generation and availability. As a result, obligations are aligned with the timing of income generation rather than the timing of access. When the delay is present, this alignment fails. The system encounters periods in which obligations must be met without access to the income that has been earned but not yet received.

This misalignment produces timing gaps that are not visible when income is evaluated in aggregate. Reported income may suggest that sufficient resources exist to meet obligations, but access to those resources is constrained by the delay. The system therefore experiences periods of strain in which it must operate without the benefit of newly earned income. These periods may be brief or extended, depending on the structure of the delay, but they represent a breakdown in the continuity of usable flow. The system's stability is compromised not by the absence of income, but by the absence of access.

As these timing gaps repeat, they accumulate into a pattern of instability. Each instance of delayed access requires the system to rely on existing resources to bridge the gap. If the delays are consistent and predictable, the system can maintain a stable bridging structure. If the delays are inconsistent or increasing, the bridging requirement expands, reducing the system's capacity to absorb further gaps. Over time, the accumulation of these requirements shifts the system from a state of continuity to a state of persistent misalignment, in which access to income no longer coincides with the timing of obligations.

The progression from delay to instability follows a defined sequence. A delay introduces a gap between earning and access. This gap creates a mismatch between when resources are generated and when they can be used. Repeated mismatches form a pattern of timing gaps, in which obligations and access are consistently misaligned. As these gaps accumulate, the system's reliance on prior resources increases, and its capacity to maintain continuity diminishes. The final state is one in which the system cannot sustain its operations without structural adjustment, because the timing of access no longer supports the timing of obligations.

Over extended time horizons, even small delays can become structural features of the system. A delay that appears negligible in isolation may, through repetition, define the baseline offset between earning and access. This offset becomes embedded in the system's operation, shaping how resources are allocated and how continuity is maintained. When the delay changes, either in length or consistency, the system must adjust to a new offset. If the adjustment cannot be absorbed, the change introduces instability. The cumulative effect of delays therefore determines how the system evolves over time.

The contrast between immediate-access systems and delayed-access systems illustrates the role of timing in stability. In an immediate-access system, the transition from earning to availability occurs with minimal delay. Income is rapidly converted into usable resources, allowing the system to align inflows with obligations. The continuity of the system is supported by the proximity of earning and access. In a delayed-access system, this proximity is replaced by separation. The system must operate across a gap, relying on prior availability to sustain operations. The larger and more variable this gap, the greater the strain on continuity.

Alignment between inflow timing and access timing determines whether income can function as a stable input. In a system where earning and access are closely aligned, the flow of income translates directly into usable resources. In a system where they are misaligned, the flow of income is partially inaccessible at critical intervals. This misalignment introduces variability into cash flow that is not present in the income flow itself. The system must therefore manage two layers of variability: one in the generation of income and another in the timing of access. Stability depends on the interaction of these layers, not on the magnitude of income alone.

Access timing defines availability windows within the system. These windows represent the periods during which income is usable. Outside these windows, income may exist in an earned state but cannot be deployed. The structure and frequency of these windows determine how the system can operate. Narrow or irregular windows restrict access, creating periods in which obligations must be met without corresponding inflow. Wider and more consistent windows provide greater continuity, allowing the system to maintain alignment between inflows and outflows. The configuration of these windows is therefore central to the system's behavior.

As the system evolves, the relationship between income and cash flow becomes a defining factor in its stability. Income generation establishes the potential for inflow, but cash flow determines whether that potential is realized in usable form. The transformation from income to cash flow is mediated by timing, and this mediation introduces both structure and risk. When the timing of access is stable and aligned, the system can sustain continuity. When it is unstable or misaligned, the system experiences repeated interruptions that accumulate into instability.

The evaluation of income must therefore extend beyond its magnitude and pattern to include its accessibility. The distinction between earned and usable value determines whether the system can operate continuously. Variability in income generation affects how much value is created, while variability in access timing affects when that value can be used. Predictability in both dimensions determines whether the system can anticipate and align with these patterns. Continuity depends on the consistent conversion of income into accessible resources across time.

As the distinction between income and cash flow becomes more pronounced, the system's dependence on access rather than generation becomes structurally dominant. Income defines potential, but cash flow defines operation. A system may generate sufficient income across a period to satisfy its obligations in aggregate, yet still experience repeated interruptions if that income is not accessible at the required intervals. The constraint on the system is therefore not the amount of income produced, but the timing with which that income becomes usable. This constraint governs how the system functions at each point in time, independent of the total value that has been earned.

Over successive periods, this distinction reshapes how stability is determined. Variability in income generation introduces uncertainty in how much value will be created, but variability in access timing introduces uncertainty in when that value can be deployed. When these uncertainties interact, the system is exposed not only to fluctuations in magnitude, but also to discontinuities in availability. The sequence through which income is converted into cash flow becomes the defining pathway through which continuity is either maintained or disrupted. Stability, in this sense, is not preserved by the presence of income, but by the consistent transformation of income into accessible resources at the moments they are required.

Within this framework, cash flow emerges as the operative form of income within the financial system. It represents the portion of income that has crossed the boundary from earning to access and is available to sustain operations. The stability of the system is therefore determined by the behavior of cash flow, not by the total amount of income earned. Income may exist in substantial quantities, but if it is not accessible when needed, it does not contribute to continuity. The system responds to availability, not to accumulation.

The separation between income and cash flow clarifies that stability is governed by usable flow rather than reported totals. The temporal structure that determines when income becomes accessible determines whether the system can maintain alignment with its obligations. Variability, predictability, and continuity must be evaluated at the level of access, not at the level of earning. Only when income is observed as it transitions into usable form can its role in maintaining stability be fully understood.

Stability vs Amount

Income is often interpreted through magnitude because magnitude is the most visible property of a financial inflow. It can be counted, reported, compared, and ranked without reference to how that inflow behaves across time. This creates a strong tendency to treat income level as a proxy for financial stability. The assumption appears intuitive. A larger inflow seems to imply greater capacity, and greater capacity appears to imply greater resilience. The error begins in the substitution. Magnitude describes how much income enters a system. Stability describes how reliably that income can support the system across successive periods. These are separate variables. One refers to scale. The other refers to behavior.

The distinction matters because a household financial system does not interact with income as an abstract total. It interacts with income as a sequence of usable inflows distributed across time. Stability is therefore not determined by the highest value the sequence can reach, but by the degree to which the sequence remains predictable. High magnitude can coexist with interruption, irregularity, and sharp fluctuation. Lower magnitude can coexist with continuity, timing consistency, and repeatability. The scale of income may affect the size of the inflow, but it does not determine whether that inflow arrives in a form the system can rely on.

Magnitude and stability are frequently conflated because magnitude can conceal instability. When income reaches high levels, the system appears buffered by the size of the inflow. Variability remains present, but it is often interpreted as less significant because the peaks are large. A volatile sequence that includes substantial inflows may still be experienced as strong when viewed through isolated periods or reported totals. The size of the peaks draws attention away from the instability of the intervals between them. This creates a distorted reading of the system, in which magnitude is mistaken for continuity.

A lower income sequence is often interpreted in the opposite way. Because the inflow is smaller, it is assumed to be structurally weaker. Yet a lower sequence can exhibit properties that make it more stable than a larger one. If timing is consistent, amount is predictable, and continuity is preserved across periods, the system can operate with a high degree of reliability. Stability does not require a large inflow. It requires that the inflow behave in a way the system can anticipate and absorb over time. The difference between these conditions shows why income level and stability cannot be treated as interchangeable concepts.

The contrast becomes clearer when income is separated into peak values and consistent patterns. Peak values indicate the maximum level an income sequence can reach. Consistency indicates the degree to which that sequence repeats without major disruption. A sequence with high peaks and wide fluctuations may produce a greater total over time than a flatter sequence, but the greater total does not make the sequence more stable. Stability depends on whether future periods resemble prior periods closely enough for the system to maintain continuity. Peaks increase magnitude. They do not resolve irregularity.

When income is examined over time, a smooth, predictable pattern and a volatile pattern behave very differently even if their totals appear similar. The smooth pattern supports continuity because each period resembles the next within a narrow range. The volatile pattern introduces uncertainty because each period may differ materially from the one before it. The system must then absorb not only variation in amount, but also variation in timing, expectation, and continuity. The result is that the same total income can produce two different stability outcomes depending on the pattern through which it is delivered.

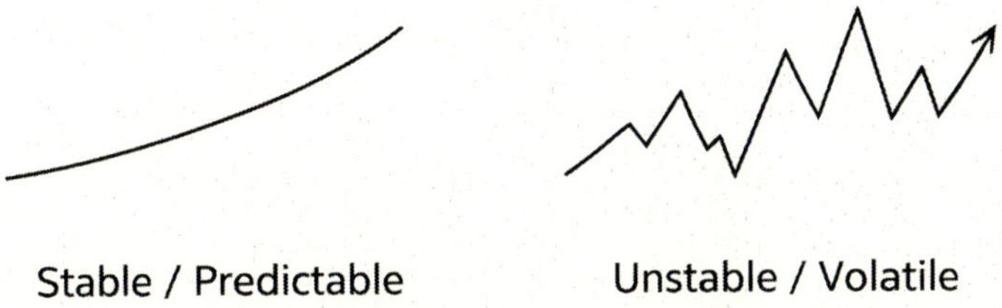

Figure 3 – Stable vs Unstable Income

This is why predictability has greater structural importance than magnitude. Predictability allows future inflows to be treated as part of an expected sequence rather than as isolated events. The system can align its obligations with an income pattern that repeats. When predictability is absent, the system cannot rely on future inflows in the same way, regardless of how large some prior inflows may have been. Large values become episodic rather than structural. They may raise the average, but they do not provide continuity.

The misconception that more income automatically creates more stability also persists because aggregated measurement compresses variation. A high annual income can be reported as a single figure, and that figure carries an implicit suggestion of enduring capacity. What disappears in that representation is the distribution of income across the year. Wide fluctuations between months, delayed receipt, interrupted contracts, or clustered payments can all exist within the same reported total. The larger the total, the easier it becomes for these fluctuations to remain unnoticed in the summary. Magnitude therefore not only fails to produce stability by itself; it can also obscure the absence of stability by making variability less visible.

This masking effect is especially strong when high inflows are intermittent. Intermittent income can elevate the total while weakening the pattern. The system then appears strong in aggregate but unstable in operation. A large inflow may temporarily increase available resources, but if the next inflow is uncertain in timing or amount, the system cannot treat the previous peak as evidence of future continuity. Stability depends on whether the pattern repeats, not on whether a prior period reached an elevated level. A single strong period does not stabilize the sequence that follows it.

By contrast, lower income that repeats with narrow variation creates a pattern the system can absorb and anticipate. The predictability of the sequence reduces uncertainty in how future periods are likely to behave. This does not increase magnitude, but it strengthens continuity. A smaller sequence that remains consistent across time often supports more reliable system behavior than a larger sequence that expands and contracts unpredictably. The reason is structural. Continuity requires repeatable inflow behavior. A system can adapt to a lower level more effectively than it can adapt to an unstable pattern whose future state is unclear.

The difference between short-term spikes and long-term consistency further separates amount from stability. Short-term spikes increase observed income in isolated periods. Long-term consistency shapes the actual operating environment of the system. A spike may alter the average, but it does not establish a repeatable pattern unless it recurs within a stable sequence. When income depends heavily on spikes, the system becomes exposed to gaps between elevated periods. Those gaps define the continuity problem. A long run of moderate, predictable inflows can support ongoing operation more effectively than a series built around occasional peaks and uncertain intervals.

This contrast reveals that the relevant unit of analysis is not the largest inflow, but the pattern formed across many inflows. A sequence with narrow variation provides information about what future periods are likely to look like. A sequence with wide variation provides much less information, even if its total is greater. The ability to form reliable expectations is central to stability because continuity depends on the relation between current conditions and expected future conditions. Magnitude can enlarge a period. Pattern determines whether periods connect.

The planning implications follow directly from this distinction. A system organized around predictable inflows can align its obligations with a reliable sequence. A system organized around volatile inflows cannot do so with the same confidence because the relationship between one period and the next is unstable. The problem is not only that income may decline. The problem is that the pattern itself cannot be treated as durable. When the sequence is volatile, each period carries a higher degree of uncertainty regarding timing, amount, or both. This uncertainty weakens continuity even when high inflows remain possible.

High income can therefore generate false confidence when its magnitude is interpreted as structural security. The system appears protected because the income level is large, but that protection depends on whether the level persists in a repeatable way. If the sequence is volatile, the appearance of strength rests on values that may not recur on schedule or at the same scale. The system may be calibrated to the visible peaks while remaining exposed to the intervals of contraction between them. In this case, magnitude does not remove fragility. It conceals it.

The fragility remains hidden because volatility is often tolerated as long as the peaks remain impressive. Attention stays fixed on the upper range of the sequence rather than on the continuity of the full pattern. This changes how instability is interpreted. Instead of being recognized as a structural property of the flow, instability is treated as a temporary deviation within an otherwise strong income profile. The result is that irregularity becomes normalized. The system is then read through its best periods rather than its repeatable periods. Stability, however, is determined by what repeats, not by what occasionally occurs.

A lower stable income sequence does not create this distortion because its behavior is easier to observe directly. The limited range of variation makes its pattern visible. The system can be understood through continuity rather than through peak impressions. This does not mean lower income is superior in magnitude. It means the stability properties of that income are easier to preserve when the pattern is narrow, repeatable, and durable. Stability emerges from the reduction of uncertainty across periods. Predictability is the mechanism through which that reduction occurs.

The relationship between volatility and continuity is decisive here. Volatility does not merely change the amount received in any one period. It alters the reliability of the sequence as a whole. When variation becomes large, future periods become harder to infer from present ones. The system loses the ability to treat prior inflows as a dependable guide to future inflows. Continuity weakens because the pattern no longer provides a stable basis for expectation. A high-income volatile sequence may still generate large totals, but its instability lies in the uncertainty attached to those totals from one period to the next.

Over multiple periods, stable patterns tend to exert greater structural influence than isolated high values. The reason is cumulative. A predictable sequence reinforces continuity every time it repeats. Each period confirms the pattern and reduces uncertainty about the next. A volatile sequence does the opposite. Each sharp change weakens the reliability of inference and increases uncertainty about future behavior. Even when the volatile sequence produces a greater total over a long interval, the continuity cost remains embedded in its pattern. Stability is shaped by repeated confirmation, not by occasional elevation.

This is why the statement that more income creates more stability cannot hold as a general rule. It may be true only when the additional income preserves or improves predictability, timing consistency, and continuity. If the increase in magnitude arrives through a more volatile pattern, the added amount and the reduced stability move in opposite directions. The larger sequence may contain more income and less continuity at the same time. Without separating these dimensions, the system is misread. What appears stronger in scale may be weaker in operation.

The deeper issue is that magnitude is visible immediately, while stability is visible only across time. A large inflow can be observed in a single period. Stability requires observation of repeated periods and their relation to one another. This difference in observability makes amount easier to privilege, even though it is the less informative variable when evaluating system behavior. Magnitude answers how much occurred. Stability answers whether the pattern can be relied upon to continue. For continuity, the second question is more important than the first.

Stability therefore operates as a constraint on how income can be used, not simply as a description of how much income exists. A system does not deploy income based on its highest observed value, but on the degree to which future inflows can be treated as reliable. When that reliability is absent, the usable capacity of income contracts, even if magnitude remains elevated.

Once this distinction is made clearly, the misconception begins to break. High income is not rejected as irrelevant. It is repositioned. Magnitude matters as a property of inflow size, but it does not define the stability of the sequence. Stability depends on whether the system can rely on the pattern through which income arrives. A lower sequence with stable repetition may support continuity more effectively than a larger sequence marked by unpredictable shifts. The decisive factor is not the height of the inflow, but the reliability of its recurrence.

The system link follows directly from this. Predictability governs whether future inflows can be treated as dependable. Dependable inflows support continuity because the system can remain aligned across successive periods. When predictability weakens, continuity weakens with it, regardless of how high some inflows may be. Stability therefore emerges from consistent patterns rather than high values. Amount can enlarge the scale of income, but only pattern determines whether that scale behaves in a stable form across time.

Income as a System Under Pressure

Income does not operate in isolation within a household financial system. It functions as one component within a structure defined by inflows, outflows, and the mechanisms that mediate the timing between them. Income represents the inflow of resources into the system. Expenses represent the structured outflow of those resources over time. Liquidity exists between these two elements as the buffer that absorbs differences in timing and magnitude. Stability is not determined by any one of these components independently. It emerges from how they interact across time and how they respond when conditions shift.

The system can be understood as a continuous process rather than a static arrangement. Income enters at intervals that may be consistent or variable. Expenses exit according to schedules that are often fixed or semi-fixed. Liquidity holds resources within the system, allowing it to operate across periods in which inflow and outflow are not aligned. These elements are interdependent. Income provides the input that sustains the system, expenses define the rate and structure of depletion, and liquidity determines whether mismatches between the two can be absorbed without interruption. The system's behavior is therefore defined by interaction, not by isolated properties.

The interaction begins with timing. Income must meet expenses across successive periods, but the timing of these two processes is rarely identical. Expenses are typically distributed at defined intervals, creating continuous demand on the system. Income may arrive in discrete events that do not align with these intervals. The difference between when income arrives and when expenses occur creates a gap. Liquidity exists to bridge this gap, allowing the system to function despite the misalignment. When the timing of inflows and outflows is closely aligned, the demand on liquidity is minimal. When the misalignment widens, liquidity becomes the primary mechanism that sustains continuity.

Alignment and misalignment define the system's operating state. In an aligned state, inflows arrive in a pattern that corresponds closely with the timing of outflows. The system operates with minimal strain, as income replenishes resources near the points at which they are required. In a misaligned state, inflows and outflows diverge in timing or magnitude. Expenses may persist while income is delayed or reduced. Liquidity must then absorb the difference, sustaining the system until inflows resume. The degree of misalignment determines the level of strain placed on liquidity and, by extension, on the system as a whole.

Pressure emerges when the mismatch between required outflow and available inflow becomes significant. This mismatch can occur through delayed income, where inflows arrive later than expected, or through variable income, where the magnitude of inflows changes across periods. It can also arise from the structure of expenses, particularly when they are fixed and cannot adjust in response to changes in inflow timing. Pressure is not defined by the absence of income, but by the relationship between when resources are needed and when they are available. It is a condition created by differences in timing and magnitude within the system.

Pressure is a signal of system stress rather than an immediate indication of failure. When a mismatch occurs, the system enters a state in which liquidity must compensate for the difference between inflow and outflow. If liquidity is sufficient, the system continues to operate without visible disruption. The pressure is absorbed internally, and the system remains intact. This absorption does not eliminate the mismatch. It defers its impact by drawing on stored resources. The presence of pressure indicates that the system is operating under conditions in which its components are not fully aligned, even if continuity is maintained.

The behavior of pressure depends on its duration and frequency. A brief mismatch that is quickly resolved places limited strain on the system. Liquidity absorbs the gap, and subsequent inflows restore balance. A sustained mismatch extends the period during which liquidity must compensate for the absence or reduction of inflow. As duration increases, the demand on liquidity intensifies. Repeated mismatches compound this effect, as each instance reduces the available buffer before the next occurs. The system transitions from managing isolated instances of pressure to operating under persistent strain.

Variability in income amplifies this dynamic. When inflows are inconsistent, the timing and magnitude of pressure become less predictable. The system cannot rely on a stable pattern of replenishment, and liquidity must absorb not only the mismatch but also the uncertainty surrounding future inflows. Fixed expenses intensify this effect because they maintain constant demand on the system regardless of inflow conditions. The combination of variable income and fixed outflows creates a structure in which pressure can arise frequently and with varying intensity. The system's stability then depends on whether liquidity can absorb these variations over time.

As pressure persists, it begins to propagate through the system. The initial effect of a mismatch is localized to the interaction between inflow and outflow. Liquidity absorbs the difference, maintaining continuity. As liquidity is drawn down, its capacity to absorb subsequent mismatches diminishes. The system becomes more sensitive to additional disruptions because the buffer that once mitigated them has been reduced. The instability that originates in the income stream does not remain confined to that stream. It spreads to the liquidity component, altering the system's ability to manage future mismatches.

As this capacity declines, the system's behavior changes in ways that are not immediately visible in aggregate measures. Early in the process, mismatches are absorbed with minimal disruption, and the system appears stable despite underlying strain. As liquidity continues to contract, each subsequent mismatch carries greater operational consequence. The system transitions from absorbing differences quietly to reacting to them more directly. Timing gaps that were previously contained begin to affect continuity, and variability in income becomes more immediately reflected in the system's functioning. The change is not in the presence of mismatch, but in the system's ability to conceal it.

This propagation creates a feedback loop. Reduced liquidity increases the system's exposure to timing mismatches, as fewer resources are available to bridge gaps. Increased exposure leads to greater sensitivity to variability in income and to the structure of expenses. Each additional mismatch exerts a larger impact because the system has less capacity to absorb it. The interaction between components becomes more constrained, and the system moves closer to a state in which continuity cannot be maintained without adjustment. The initial instability in income thus transforms into broader system instability through its effect on liquidity.

The propagation of instability is not linear. Early stages of pressure may have limited visible impact because liquidity provides sufficient buffering. As liquidity declines, each subsequent mismatch has a greater effect. The system's response becomes more constrained, and the margin for absorbing variability narrows. The progression from stability to instability is therefore gradual at first and accelerates as the buffer is depleted. This acceleration reflects the interdependence of the system's components. Changes in one element alter the conditions under which the others operate.

Failure occurs when liquidity can no longer absorb the mismatch between inflow and outflow. At this point, the system reaches a state in which obligations cannot be met within the existing structure. The breakdown is not the result of a single event but the culmination of repeated pressure that has not been resolved. Each instance of mismatch contributes to the depletion of the buffer, and the accumulation of these instances eventually exceeds the system's capacity to compensate. The failure is therefore structural. It arises from the interaction of components over time rather than from an isolated disruption.

This distinction is critical because it shifts the interpretation of instability from event-driven to process-driven. A single disruption may initiate pressure, but it does not determine the outcome. The outcome depends on how the system responds to that pressure and whether it can restore alignment between inflow and outflow. When mismatches are infrequent and liquidity is sufficient, the system absorbs and recovers. When mismatches are frequent or sustained, and liquidity is progressively reduced, the system moves toward breakdown. The path to failure is defined by repeated unresolved pressure, not by the presence of any one disruption.

The role of expenses in this process is often less visible but equally important. Expenses define the rate at which resources leave the system. When expenses are structured in a fixed manner, they create constant demand that does not adjust in response to variability in income. This rigidity increases the likelihood of mismatch when inflows are delayed or reduced. Even in the absence of increased expenses, the persistence of outflows ensures that any delay in inflow produces pressure. The interaction between fixed outflows and variable inflows is therefore a central source of system stress.

Liquidity functions as the mediator of this interaction. It determines whether the system can sustain operations when inflow and outflow are not aligned. Its presence allows the system to operate across periods of mismatch, but its capacity is finite. Each instance of pressure draws on this capacity, and without sufficient replenishment, the buffer diminishes. The effectiveness of liquidity is therefore contingent on the balance between the frequency and duration of mismatches and the rate at which inflows restore the buffer. This balance defines whether the system can maintain continuity under pressure.

The system can be understood as a loop in which each component influences the others. Income provides the input that replenishes liquidity. Expenses draw from liquidity, creating the demand that must be met. Liquidity absorbs the differences between the timing and magnitude of these processes. When income is stable and aligned with expenses, liquidity remains relatively constant. When income is variable or delayed, liquidity fluctuates as it absorbs mismatches. These fluctuations feed back into the system, altering its capacity to manage subsequent interactions.

The presence of pressure reveals the structure of this loop. Under stable conditions, the interactions between components may appear smooth, and the system operates without visible strain. When pressure arises, the underlying relationships become more apparent. The dependence of expenses on inflow timing, the role of liquidity in bridging gaps, and the propagation of instability across components are all exposed. Pressure therefore serves as a diagnostic condition. It does not create the system's structure, but it makes the system's behavior visible.

As pressure scales from small mismatches to sustained misalignment, the system's state changes. A small mismatch may be absorbed with minimal impact on liquidity, leaving the system largely unchanged. Sustained mismatch requires continuous absorption, reducing liquidity over time and altering the system's ability to respond to future conditions. The transition from small to sustained pressure marks a shift from temporary imbalance to structural strain. The system moves from a state in which it can easily recover to one in which recovery becomes increasingly difficult as the buffer diminishes.

The interaction between components under these conditions determines whether the system remains stable. Stability is not a property of income alone, nor of expenses, nor of liquidity. It is a property of how these elements function together across time. A system with stable income but poorly aligned expenses may experience pressure due to timing mismatches. A system with variable income but sufficient liquidity may maintain continuity despite fluctuations. The outcome depends on the configuration and interaction of all components, not on the condition of any single element.

This interdependence establishes that stability must be evaluated at the system level. Income contributes to stability by providing inflow, but it does not determine stability independently. Expenses shape the demand placed on the system, and liquidity determines whether mismatches can be absorbed. The interaction of these components under conditions of alignment and misalignment defines whether the system can sustain operations. Pressure reveals the points at which this interaction becomes strained, and propagation shows how instability spreads when that strain is not resolved.

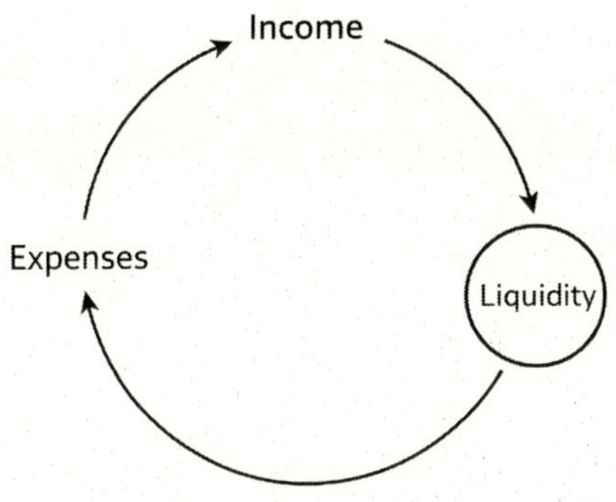

Figure 4 – Income System Loop

Variability, Volatility, and Predictability

Income behaves across time through variation in both magnitude and timing. These variations are not deviations from a baseline state; they are inherent properties of how income is generated and received. Magnitude varies as the amount of each inflow changes across periods. Timing varies as the intervals between inflows expand, contract, or shift. Together, these dimensions define the behavioral structure of income. Any analysis of stability must begin with the recognition that variability is not an exception to be filtered out, but a structural condition that must be understood.

Variation in magnitude describes how income fluctuates in size from one period to the next. These fluctuations may be narrow, with each inflow remaining close to a central value, or wide, with inflows differing substantially. Variation in timing describes how the spacing between inflows changes. Intervals may be consistent, producing a regular cadence, or irregular, producing gaps or clustering. These two axes operate independently. Income can exhibit stable timing with variable amounts, or stable amounts with irregular timing. It can also vary across both dimensions simultaneously. The interaction of these variations forms the observable pattern of income over time.

The independence of these two axes creates combinations of behavior that are not immediately apparent when income is evaluated in aggregate. A sequence with stable magnitude but irregular timing may produce the same total as one with stable timing and variable magnitude, yet the operational experience of each differs. When timing is irregular, the spacing between inflows becomes the dominant source of uncertainty, even if the amounts themselves remain consistent. When magnitude varies but timing remains stable, the system encounters fluctuations in scale rather than in availability. These distinctions illustrate that variability is not a single dimension, but a composite of interacting behaviors that shape how income is experienced across time.

Variability exists along a spectrum. At one end, income exhibits low variability, with both magnitude and timing remaining within a narrow range. The sequence appears smooth, with each period resembling the next. At the other end, income exhibits high variability, with both dimensions fluctuating widely. The sequence becomes uneven, with significant differences between adjacent periods. Between these extremes lie intermediate states in which one dimension remains stable while the other varies. This spectrum does not define stability directly. It defines the range within which income behavior can occur.

The presence of variability does not, by itself, determine whether income is stable or unstable. A sequence with limited variation may appear stable, but if its pattern is inconsistent or shifts over time, predictability is reduced. A sequence with substantial variation may still exhibit stability if the variation follows a recognizable pattern. The critical distinction lies not in how much variation exists, but in how that variation is structured. Stability depends on whether the sequence forms a pattern that can be anticipated, not on whether variation is minimized.

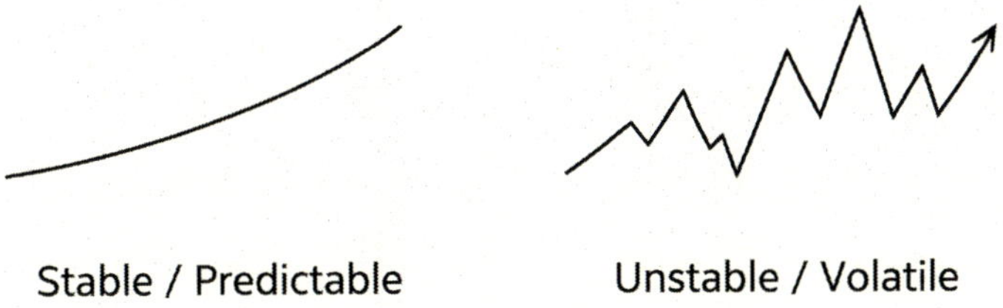

Figure 5 – Stable vs Unstable Income

The interpretation of variability therefore requires attention to pattern. A smooth sequence suggests that both magnitude and timing vary within narrow bounds, producing a pattern that is easy to anticipate. A jagged sequence indicates wider variation, but the key question is whether that variation follows a consistent structure or appears irregular. When variation is structured, even if pronounced, the sequence can be understood as patterned. When variation is unstructured, the sequence becomes difficult to interpret, and future behavior cannot be inferred from past behavior.

Volatility emerges when variability lacks a reliable pattern. It is not defined solely by the presence of large fluctuations, but by the absence of consistent structure within those fluctuations. A sequence may exhibit high variability but remain predictable if the variation follows a repeating form. Volatility arises when the variation does not repeat in a stable way. Each period becomes less connected to the previous one, and the sequence loses coherence. The system cannot use prior observations to form expectations about future inflows because the underlying structure is unstable.

The effect of volatility is to increase uncertainty. When income varies without pattern, the range of possible outcomes in future periods expands. Both magnitude and timing become less certain, and the system cannot rely on established sequences to anticipate inflows. This uncertainty affects how continuity is maintained, as the relationship between current and future conditions weakens. Volatility disrupts the ability to treat income as a repeatable process. Instead, each period must be interpreted in isolation, reducing the system's capacity to maintain alignment across time.

Predictability represents the opposite condition. It is the ability to anticipate future inflows based on observed patterns in prior periods. Predictability does not require the absence of variation. It requires that variation occur within a structure that repeats or evolves in a consistent way. A sequence with predictable variation allows the system to form expectations about both magnitude and timing. These expectations need not be exact. They must be sufficiently reliable to establish continuity between periods. Predictability therefore depends on the presence of pattern, not on the elimination of fluctuation.

The distinction between predictable variability and volatility is central. Predictable variability describes a sequence in which changes occur, but those changes follow a recognizable form. This form may include cycles, ranges, or recurring intervals that allow the sequence to be interpreted as structured. Volatility describes a sequence in which changes occur without such structure. The difference lies in whether the variation contributes to a coherent pattern or disrupts it. In one case, variation is integrated into the system's behavior. In the other, it fragments that behavior.

Income forms sequences across time, and these sequences are the basis for pattern formation. Each inflow contributes to a series that can be observed and analyzed for repetition, consistency, and structure. Patterns emerge when the sequence exhibits regularity in how magnitude and timing interact. This regularity may take the form of consistent intervals, bounded ranges, or recurring fluctuations. When such patterns are present, the sequence becomes interpretable. The system can relate current inflows to prior ones and use that relationship to anticipate future behavior.

Pattern formation depends on repetition. A single observation does not establish a pattern. Multiple observations across successive periods are required to determine whether variation is structured or unstructured. As the sequence extends, the presence or absence of repetition becomes clearer. Structured variability reveals itself through recurring forms, while unstructured variability reveals itself through inconsistency. The distinction between these two states determines whether the sequence can support predictability.

As the sequence extends across more periods, the distinction between structured and unstructured variation becomes more pronounced. In a structured sequence, repetition reinforces the pattern, allowing deviations to be interpreted within an established range. In an unstructured sequence, additional observations do not clarify the pattern but instead expand the range of possible outcomes. The system gains confidence in one case and loses it in the other. This divergence reflects the difference between variability that is bounded and variability that is effectively random. Bounded variation allows expectations to stabilize over time, while unbounded variation prevents expectations from forming.

Structured variability supports predictability because it provides a stable reference for expectation. Even when magnitude fluctuates or timing shifts, the recurrence of these changes within a defined pattern allows the system to anticipate their occurrence. Unstructured variability undermines predictability because it removes this reference. Without a stable pattern, each period becomes less informative about the next. The sequence loses continuity, and the system cannot rely on past behavior to guide future expectations.

The relationship between variability, volatility, and predictability defines the behavior axis of income. Variability describes the extent of change in magnitude and timing. Volatility describes the absence of structure within that change. Predictability describes the presence of structure that allows future behavior to be anticipated. These concepts are interdependent. Variability is the underlying condition. Volatility and predictability describe how that condition is organized. Stability depends on whether variability is organized into patterns that can be relied upon.

When variability reduces predictability, it becomes destabilizing. The system loses its ability to anticipate inflows, and continuity weakens. When variability is structured and predictable, it does not necessarily reduce stability. It may introduce fluctuation, but the system can adapt to that fluctuation because it follows a recognizable form. The distinction lies in how variation affects the relationship between periods. Predictable patterns maintain that relationship. Volatile patterns disrupt it.

This framework clarifies that stability is not achieved by minimizing variation alone. A sequence with low variation but shifting structure may be less predictable than a sequence with higher variation but stable patterning. The presence of variation is not the defining factor. The organization of that variation determines whether the sequence supports continuity. Predictability becomes the dominant variable because it governs whether variation can be integrated into a stable pattern.

As income behavior is observed over extended periods, the role of pattern becomes more pronounced. Short sequences may appear stable or unstable based on limited observations, but longer sequences reveal whether variation is structured. Repetition confirms pattern, while inconsistency reveals volatility. The accumulation of observations strengthens or weakens predictability depending on how the sequence evolves. Stability is therefore a property that emerges over time, as the behavior of income reveals its underlying structure.

The connection to system behavior follows directly. Variability influences predictability by shaping how consistent the sequence is across periods. Predictability influences continuity by determining whether the system can rely on future inflows. Continuity, in turn, determines stability by maintaining alignment across time. When variability is structured, predictability remains intact, continuity is preserved, and stability is supported. When variability becomes unstructured, predictability declines, continuity weakens, and stability deteriorates.

As predictability declines, the system's ability to treat income as a continuous process begins to contract. Without a stable pattern, each inflow loses its connection to the sequence that precedes it. The system cannot extend assumptions forward because there is no reliable structure to extend. This does not only increase uncertainty; it alters how income functions within the system. Instead of operating as a stream that supports continuity across periods, income becomes a series of isolated events. Each event may contribute resources, but it does not reinforce a pattern that can sustain alignment over time. The distinction is subtle but structural. Predictable income behaves as part of a sequence. Unpredictable income behaves as a collection of occurrences. Stability depends on the presence of the former, not the latter.

Income stability is therefore not defined by the absence of variation or by the magnitude of inflows. It is defined by whether the sequence of income exhibits patterns that can be anticipated and relied upon. Variability is always present, but it becomes destabilizing only when it disrupts pattern formation. Predictability emerges as the organizing principle that determines whether variation contributes to stability or undermines it.

Timing and Sequence Risk

Income and expenses do not exist as aggregated quantities within a household financial system. They exist as sequences of events distributed across time. Each inflow occurs at a specific moment, and each obligation requires fulfillment at a specific moment. These moments form ordered sequences, and the system operates through the interaction of these sequences. Stability depends on whether the order of inflows aligns with the order of required outflows. When alignment is preserved, continuity is maintained. When alignment breaks, the system encounters sequence risk.

Timing mismatch occurs when the arrival of income does not coincide with the occurrence of obligations. Sequence risk arises when the order of these events produces gaps in which obligations must be met before the corresponding inflow is available. These conditions are not defined by the total amount of income or the total amount of expenses. They are defined by the arrangement of events in time. A system may generate sufficient income over a period, yet still fail to meet obligations if the sequence of inflows does not align with the sequence of outflows. Totals do not determine system function. Order does.

The structure of income as a sequence of discrete inflows introduces inherent variability in timing. Income arrives at intervals that may be regular or irregular, but it is not continuous. Expenses, by contrast, often follow fixed or semi-fixed schedules. They create a series of required outflows that must be met at defined points. This difference in structure means that mismatch is not an anomaly. It is a natural consequence of how inflows and outflows are organized. The system must therefore operate across the differences in these sequences, and its stability depends on whether those differences are manageable.

Order dependency defines how the system responds to these sequences. Each event in the sequence is evaluated in relation to the events that precede it. An obligation that occurs before an inflow must be met without the benefit of that inflow. An inflow that arrives after an obligation cannot retroactively resolve the gap created by that obligation. The system does not evaluate income and expenses as a combined total at the end of a period. It evaluates each event in the order it occurs. The outcome of the system is therefore determined by the sequence, not by the sum.

This introduces an asymmetry within the system that cannot be neutralized by later events. Once an obligation has occurred without the required resources, the sequence has already diverged from continuity. Subsequent inflows may restore available resources, but they do not restore the order in which events occurred. The system does not reset. It carries forward the consequence of the mismatch. This irreversibility distinguishes sequence failure from aggregate shortfall. In an aggregate shortfall, additional income can compensate for prior deficiency. In a sequence failure, compensation arrives out of order and therefore does not resolve the original disruption. The system remains altered by the timing of the event, not by the total that follows.

Sequence mismatch becomes visible when inflows and outflows are placed on the same timeline. Obligations appear as evenly spaced or fixed points, while income appears as discrete arrivals that may not align with those points. When an obligation occurs before the next inflow, a gap emerges. This gap represents a period in which the system must function without access to incoming resources. The presence of such gaps defines timing mismatch. The frequency and duration of these gaps define the level of sequence risk within the system.

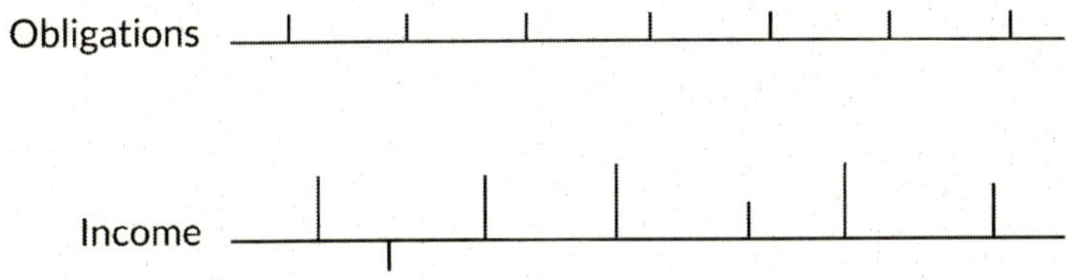

Figure 6 – Timing Mismatch

The behavior of sequence mismatch over time determines whether the system remains stable. A single gap may be absorbed without lasting impact if subsequent inflows restore alignment. However, when gaps recur, they create a pattern of misalignment. Each gap requires the system to bridge the interval between obligation and inflow. When this pattern persists, the system operates under continuous sequence pressure, in which each new obligation must be evaluated against the timing of the next inflow. The accumulation of these gaps alters the system's operating state from one of alignment to one of persistent mismatch.

Small mismatches often appear insignificant when viewed in isolation. A delay of a few days between an obligation and the corresponding inflow may not immediately disrupt the system. However, the effect of these mismatches depends on their position within the sequence. An early mismatch, occurring near the beginning of a sequence of obligations, can shift the entire sequence forward, creating additional gaps downstream. A late mismatch may compress the sequence, reducing the interval between subsequent obligations and inflows. The position of each mismatch within the sequence therefore influences how it propagates across time.

Clustering and spacing of inflows further affect sequence behavior. When income arrives in clusters, multiple inflows occur within a short interval, followed by longer gaps with no inflow. This pattern creates periods of temporary alignment followed by extended misalignment. Obligations that fall within the clustered period are easily met, while those that fall within the gap must be bridged. In contrast, evenly spaced inflows provide more consistent alignment with obligations, reducing the frequency and duration of gaps. The distribution of inflows across time therefore shapes the sequence risk profile of the system.

Sequence drift occurs when the relative timing of inflows and outflows shifts over successive periods. This drift may result from changes in when income arrives or from changes in when obligations occur. Even small shifts can accumulate, altering the alignment between sequences. A system that begins in alignment may gradually move into misalignment as the timing of inflows lags behind the timing of obligations. This drift is often subtle, as each individual shift may appear minor. Over time, however, the cumulative effect changes the structure of the sequence, increasing the frequency of gaps.

The presence of sequence risk explains why systems can fail despite sufficient aggregate income. When income is evaluated in total, it may appear that resources are adequate to meet obligations. This evaluation ignores the order in which those resources become available. If inflows occur after obligations, the system cannot use those inflows to meet obligations at the required time. The total may be sufficient, but the sequence is not. Failure occurs not because the system lacks resources in aggregate, but because it lacks resources at the moments they are required.

This distinction becomes clearer when comparing systems with identical totals but different sequences. Two systems may generate the same amount of income over a period and face the same total level of expenses. If one system receives income in a sequence that aligns with obligations, it maintains continuity. If the other receives income in a sequence that lags behind obligations, it experiences gaps. The difference in outcome is not explained by magnitude. It is explained by order. The same totals produce different results because the sequences differ.

Aggregate measures obscure this distinction because they collapse the sequence into a single value. The total income for a period does not reveal when each inflow occurred relative to obligations. It presents the system as though all resources were available simultaneously, which is not the case. This compression removes the information necessary to evaluate sequence risk. A system that appears stable in aggregate may contain multiple sequence mismatches that are not visible in the total. The instability remains hidden until it manifests as a breakdown in continuity.

Failure emerges when sequence mismatch persists to the point at which obligations cannot be met in order. Each unmet obligation represents a point at which the system has encountered a gap that cannot be bridged. The sequence is broken. Subsequent inflows may restore resources, but they cannot restore the order that has already been disrupted. The system's failure is therefore not a function of total insufficiency, but of sequence breakdown. The inability to meet obligations at the required moments defines the failure state.

As these disruptions accumulate, the system transitions from isolated sequence errors to a condition in which the sequence itself becomes unstable. Each unresolved gap alters the position of subsequent obligations relative to future inflows, increasing the likelihood of additional mismatches. The system begins to operate in a shifted state, where alignment is no longer the default condition but the exception. This creates a cascading effect in which each new event is evaluated within a sequence that has already been displaced. The instability is no longer tied to a single mismatch, but to the altered structure of the sequence itself. At this point, continuity is no longer supported by the system's arrangement, and restoration requires a change in sequence rather than an increase in total resources.

This failure is cumulative rather than instantaneous. A single mismatch may not produce immediate breakdown if the system can absorb it. However, repeated mismatches weaken the system's ability to maintain alignment. Each gap introduces a deviation from the expected sequence, and these deviations accumulate over time. The system moves from a state in which mismatches are occasional to one in which they are structural. At this point, the sequence no longer supports continuity, and failure becomes inevitable.

The role of predictability in this context is limited to pattern recognition. A predictable sequence allows the system to anticipate when inflows will occur, but predictability alone does not ensure alignment. If the predictable pattern is misaligned with the sequence of obligations, the system will consistently encounter gaps. Predictability without alignment produces a stable pattern of mismatch rather than stability. The system can anticipate the gaps, but anticipation does not eliminate them. Alignment of sequences is required for predictability to translate into continuity.

This establishes that stability requires both predictable patterns and correct ordering. Predictability provides the basis for expectation, but sequence alignment determines whether those expectations support system function. When inflows and outflows are ordered in a way that maintains continuity, the system operates smoothly. When they are ordered in a way that creates gaps, the system encounters repeated disruptions. The difference lies in how the sequences are arranged relative to one another.

Sequence risk is therefore a structural property of the system, arising from the interaction of ordered events. It cannot be resolved by increasing totals alone, as additional income does not change the order in which events occur. A system with higher income may still experience sequence mismatch if the timing of inflows does not align with obligations.

Conversely, a system with lower income may maintain continuity if its sequences are aligned. The determining factor is not the amount of income, but the arrangement of events in time.

The system responds to each event as it occurs, evaluating whether the required resources are available at that moment. This event-by-event evaluation reinforces the importance of order. The system does not defer its assessment to the end of a period. It operates continuously, responding to the sequence as it unfolds. Each obligation must be met in its position within the sequence, and each inflow contributes only when it arrives. The outcome is determined by the sequence of these interactions, not by their aggregate.

When sequence mismatch is fully understood, the relationship between timing and stability becomes clear. Stability is not a function of having sufficient income over time. It is a function of having income available at the correct moments within the sequence of obligations. Timing defines when resources can be used. Sequence defines whether those resources arrive in the order required to sustain continuity. When either condition fails, the system encounters instability regardless of total income.

The dependence on sequence establishes that stability is inherently time-based. It cannot be evaluated without reference to the order of events. Income must be analyzed as a sequence of inflows, and expenses as a sequence of outflows, with stability determined by their alignment. The system's behavior emerges from this alignment, and its failure emerges from its absence. Recognizing that order determines viability completes the transition from viewing income as a quantity to understanding it as a sequence that must be correctly arranged across time.

Income Gaps and Disruptions

Income enters a household financial system as a sequence of inflows distributed across time. When this sequence is uninterrupted, each inflow contributes to the continuity of the system. A gap occurs when one or more expected inflows are absent, creating a period in which the sequence is broken. This absence is not defined by misalignment or variability within the sequence. It is defined by the absence of inflow itself. A disruption is the structural interruption of continuity that results when the sequence ceases to deliver inflows for a period of time. The defining variable in this condition is duration. The length of time over which inflow is absent determines how the system responds.

A gap is therefore not a deviation within the sequence, but a segment where the sequence does not exist. During this segment, the system continues to operate, but without replenishment. Obligations do not pause in response to the absence of inflow. They continue according to their own sequence, creating a condition where outflows persist while inflows are temporarily or indefinitely suspended. The system must then sustain itself without new input, relying entirely on what has already been accumulated. The longer this condition persists, the more the system transitions from continuity to strain.

Gaps can be distinguished by their duration. A short gap represents a temporary interruption in the sequence. The absence of inflow is brief, and the system remains within a range where continuity can be maintained without structural change. An extended gap represents a prolonged absence, where the sequence is interrupted for a duration that alters the system's state. The distinction between these two conditions is not defined by the presence of a gap, but by how long the absence persists relative to the system's capacity to operate without replenishment. Duration determines whether the gap remains a transient condition or becomes a structural strain.

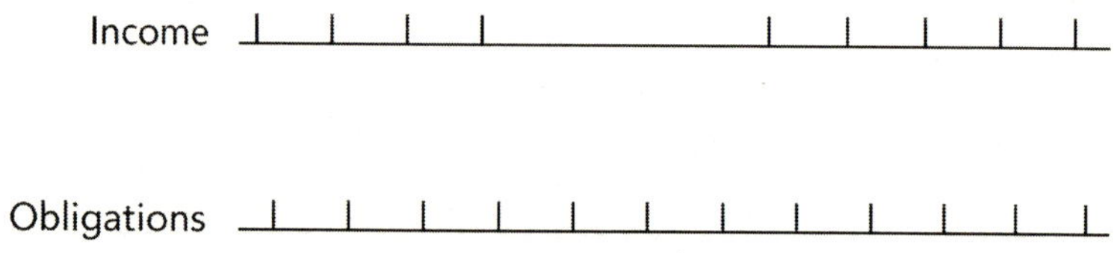

Figure 7 – Interruption Timeline

The difference between short and extended gaps becomes apparent when observing how the system behaves during the absence of inflow. In a short gap, the system experiences a temporary deviation from its normal sequence. Obligations continue, but the absence of inflow is limited in duration, allowing the system to maintain continuity until the sequence resumes. The interruption is absorbed without altering the underlying structure. In an extended gap, the absence persists beyond this threshold. The system remains without replenishment for a longer period, and the continued presence of obligations creates an increasing divergence between available resources and required outflows. The system does not pause while income is absent. It continues to function, and the absence becomes the defining condition.

This introduces a fundamental property of the system: it is time-dependent and continuous. The absence of inflow does not suspend time or obligations. Each period that passes without income increases the duration of the gap and extends the interval over which the system must operate without replenishment. The effect of this extension is cumulative. Each additional period without inflow compounds the strain introduced by the previous period. The system moves further away from its prior state of continuity as the gap lengthens.

The mechanism through which gaps affect the system is direct. Without inflow, there is no addition to available resources. Outflows continue to reduce the system's capacity, and the absence of replenishment means that this reduction is not offset. The system therefore enters a state of continuous depletion during the gap. The rate of this depletion is determined by the structure of obligations, but the presence of depletion itself is determined by the absence of inflow. The system's behavior during this period is governed entirely by duration. The longer the gap, the greater the cumulative reduction.

Over time, the difference between short and extended gaps becomes more pronounced. A short gap produces a limited period of depletion that can be reversed when inflow resumes. The system returns to its prior state with minimal lasting impact. An extended gap produces a prolonged period of depletion that changes the system's condition. The absence of inflow persists long enough to alter the system's ability to maintain continuity. The gap is no longer a temporary deviation. It becomes a structural disruption that affects subsequent periods even after inflow resumes.

The relationship between duration and instability is not linear. In the early stages of a gap, the system may absorb the absence without visible disruption. As the gap extends, each additional period without inflow increases the strain at an accelerating rate. The system's capacity to maintain continuity declines as the duration increases, and the effect of each additional period becomes more significant. This acceleration reflects the compounding nature of absence. The impact of the gap is not confined to the moment it begins. It expands over time as the duration increases.

The compounding effect of gaps arises from the interaction between absence and continuity. Each period without inflow weakens the sequence by extending the interval between inflows. The sequence becomes less dense, and the continuity that was previously maintained by regular inflows is disrupted. As the gap lengthens, the sequence loses its integrity. The system transitions from a state where inflows are expected to occur within a predictable interval to a state where the absence of inflow becomes the dominant condition. This transition marks the shift from temporary interruption to structural disruption.

Gaps do not remain isolated events within the system. Their effects extend beyond the period of absence. A short gap may leave the system largely unchanged, but an extended gap alters the system's trajectory. The absence of inflow during the gap creates a new baseline from which the system must operate. Even when inflow resumes, the system does not return to its prior state immediately. The effects of the gap persist, influencing how the system behaves in subsequent periods. The gap therefore becomes part of the system's history, shaping its future behavior.

When inflow resumes after an extended gap, the resumption does not erase the duration that preceded it. The sequence restarts, but it does not restart from the system's prior condition. The interruption has already altered the level of available resources, the position of continuing obligations, and the system's tolerance for further absence. Income returns into a structure that has been changed by the period without replenishment. For this reason, resumption should not be interpreted as restoration. It is only the end of the gap itself. The system may remain unstable even after inflow has resumed because the effects of duration continue to shape how subsequent periods are experienced.

The duration of absence functions as an instability multiplier. Each additional unit of time without inflow increases the system's exposure to failure. This exposure is not tied to the amount of income that was previously generated. It is tied to the length of time over which no new income is received. A system with high prior income may still experience significant instability if the gap is extended. The absence of inflow removes the system's primary mechanism for replenishment, and duration determines how long the system must operate without it.

The compounding nature of gaps also affects the system's sensitivity to subsequent conditions. As the gap lengthens, the system becomes more vulnerable to any additional disruptions. The absence of inflow reduces the system's ability to absorb further variation, and each additional period without income increases this vulnerability. The system's resilience declines as the duration of the gap increases, creating a condition where the threshold for failure becomes lower over time. The longer the gap persists, the less additional stress is required to produce breakdown.

Failure emerges when the duration of absence exceeds the system's capacity to sustain operations without inflow. At this point, the system can no longer maintain continuity. Obligations continue, but the absence of replenishment has reduced available resources to a level where they are insufficient to meet those obligations. The failure is not caused by misalignment or variability within the sequence. It is caused by the absence of the sequence itself. The system breaks because it has been operating without inflow for too long.

This failure mode is distinct from those based on timing or variability. It does not require mismatch between inflows and outflows, nor does it require unpredictable variation. It requires only that inflow ceases for a sufficient duration. The system may have been stable prior to the gap, with aligned sequences and predictable patterns. The introduction of an extended absence disrupts this stability by removing the inflow entirely. The system then operates under a new condition where continuity must be maintained without replenishment. The duration of this condition determines the outcome.

The contrast between short and extended gaps reinforces the role of duration. A short gap does not fundamentally alter the system because the absence is brief. The sequence is interrupted but quickly restored. An extended gap changes the system because the absence persists long enough to alter its structure. The sequence is not merely interrupted; it is replaced by a period of absence that defines the system's behavior. The difference between these two outcomes is not the presence of the gap, but its length.

The relationship between sequence and continuity becomes clearer when considering gaps. A sequence of inflows supports continuity by providing regular replenishment. A gap removes that replenishment for a period, creating a discontinuity in the sequence. The system must then operate across this discontinuity. If the gap is short, the discontinuity is limited. If the gap is extended, the discontinuity becomes the dominant feature of the sequence. The system's behavior is then defined by absence rather than by inflow.

Stability therefore depends on the system's ability to tolerate gaps within the sequence. Tolerance is defined by duration. The system can sustain continuity across short gaps, but extended gaps exceed its capacity to operate without inflow. The threshold between these two conditions is not fixed. It depends on the interaction between the system's structure and the duration of absence. What remains constant is that duration determines whether a gap is manageable or destabilizing.

The absence of inflow introduces a form of risk that is independent of magnitude and sequence alignment. It represents a condition where the system must function without its primary source of replenishment. The impact of this condition is governed by how long it persists. Duration becomes the central variable, defining how the system transitions from continuity to instability. The longer the absence, the greater the cumulative effect on the system's ability to sustain itself.

The system's behavior under interruption reveals that continuity is not guaranteed by the presence of income in aggregate or by the correct ordering of inflows and outflows. Continuity requires that inflows occur within a timeframe that maintains the sequence. When inflow ceases, even temporarily, the sequence is broken. The system must then rely on its capacity to operate without replenishment, and this capacity is limited by time. The duration of the gap determines whether continuity can be maintained or whether the system moves toward breakdown.

This establishes that stability is dependent on uninterrupted sequence or on gaps that remain within a tolerable duration. The presence of inflow must be sustained across time, or the absence must be short enough that continuity is not disrupted. When absence extends beyond this threshold, the system transitions into instability regardless of prior conditions. The determining factor is not the amount of income previously generated, but the length of time over which no new income is received. Duration defines survivability within the system, and extended absence defines its limits.

Dependency and Concentration Risk

Income does not originate as an independent flow. Each inflow is derived from an underlying source, and that source represents a point of dependency within the household financial system. Dependency defines the relationship between income and the conditions required for that income to exist. When a source is active, it produces inflow. When a source is altered or removed, the inflow associated with it changes or disappears. Income is therefore not a primary variable. It is the output of a structure composed of sources, and its stability depends on the configuration of that structure.

Dependency describes the extent to which income relies on specific sources for its existence. Each source carries conditions that determine whether it continues to produce inflow. These conditions may include contractual relationships, institutional arrangements, or other external factors that are not controlled by the system itself. The presence of dependency means that income is contingent. It exists only as long as the underlying sources remain intact and functional. The system inherits the characteristics of those sources, including their stability and their susceptibility to change.

Concentration describes how income is distributed across these sources. When income is spread across multiple sources with relatively balanced contributions, dependency is distributed. When a large portion of income is derived from a small number of sources, dependency is concentrated.

The degree of concentration determines how sensitive the system is to changes in any individual source. A distributed structure reduces the impact of any single change because no one source dominates the system. A concentrated structure amplifies the impact of change because one or a few sources account for a disproportionate share of total inflow.

The distinction between distributed and concentrated structures defines the system's exposure to disruption. In a distributed structure, each source contributes a smaller portion of total income. The system's stability is less dependent on the continuity of any one source. In a concentrated structure, a single source may account for a significant portion of total income. The system becomes highly dependent on the continuity of that source. The loss or alteration of that source introduces a change that is large relative to the system as a whole. The same event produces different outcomes depending on how income is distributed across sources.

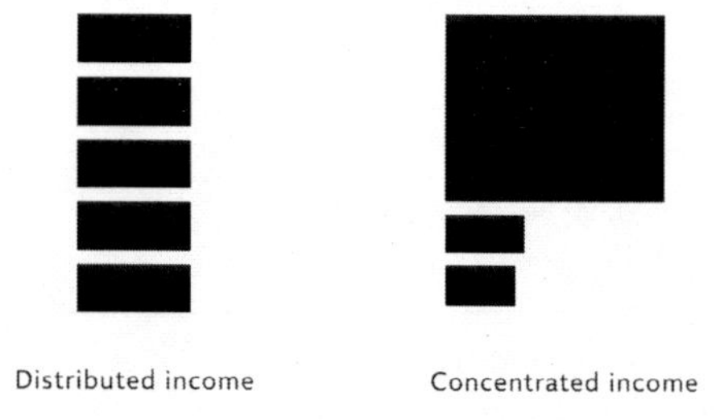

Figure 8 – Concentration Stack

The structural difference between these configurations is not visible in total income alone. Two systems may report the same aggregate income, yet differ significantly in how that income is generated. One system may derive its income from multiple balanced sources, while another derives most of its income from a single dominant source. The totals are identical, but the dependency structures are not. The system with distributed dependency can absorb the loss of any one source with limited impact on total inflow. The system with concentrated dependency cannot. The loss of its dominant source produces a change that affects the entire system.

The mechanism through which dependency creates risk is direct. Each source represents a potential point of failure. When a source changes, the inflow it produces changes accordingly. In a distributed structure, the effect of this change is proportional to the share of income associated with that source. In a concentrated structure, the effect is amplified because the share is larger. The system's exposure is therefore determined by the proportion of income that depends on each source. Concentration increases exposure by increasing the proportion associated with a single point of dependency.

This introduces the concept of single-point failure within the income structure. A single-point failure occurs when the loss of one source produces a disproportionate impact on total income. In a highly concentrated structure, the dominant source becomes a critical node. The system's stability depends heavily on its continuity. If this node fails, the system experiences a significant reduction in inflow that cannot be offset by other sources. The failure is not distributed across the system. It is concentrated at a single point, and its effect propagates through the entire structure.

The system inherits this risk from its dependencies. The characteristics of each source become characteristics of the income it generates. A source with stable conditions contributes to stability, while a source with uncertain conditions contributes to fragility. When dependency is concentrated, the system becomes highly sensitive to the characteristics of the dominant source. The stability of the entire system reflects the stability of that source. When dependency is distributed, the system reflects a combination of the characteristics of multiple sources, reducing sensitivity to any one of them.

The behavior of the system under loss reveals how concentration shapes outcomes. When a minor source is removed, the system experiences a reduction in inflow proportional to that source's contribution. The impact is limited because the majority of income remains intact. The system continues to operate with a reduced but still substantial inflow. When a major source is removed, the system experiences a reduction that is large relative to total income. The change alters the system's structure, not just its scale. The system must then operate under a fundamentally different inflow condition, as a significant portion of its income has been removed.

This difference in impact illustrates the concept of proportional sensitivity. The effect of losing a source is determined not by the absolute value of that source, but by its proportion within the overall structure. A source that represents a small percentage of total income has limited influence on system stability. A source that represents a large percentage has a dominant influence. The system's sensitivity to loss is therefore uneven. It is concentrated around the sources that contribute the largest share of income.

The uneven sensitivity introduced by concentration creates structural fragility. Fragility is defined by the system's susceptibility to large changes resulting from small shifts in underlying conditions. In a concentrated structure, a change affecting a single source can produce a large change in total income. The system's response is disproportionate to the number of sources affected. This disproportionate response is the defining characteristic of fragility. The system appears stable while the dominant source remains intact, but it contains a latent vulnerability that is exposed when that source changes.

Failure in this context does not require complex interactions between timing, sequence, or duration. It can occur through the removal or degradation of a single dependency. The system may have exhibited stable timing and predictable patterns prior to the loss. The sequence may have been aligned, and inflows may have occurred without interruption. The failure arises not from how income behaves across time, but from what that income depends on. When the dominant source is removed, the system loses a substantial portion of its inflow, and the prior conditions of stability no longer apply.

This form of failure is structural rather than temporal. It is not the result of misalignment or absence within a sequence, but of a change in the underlying structure that generates the sequence. The system's stability is compromised because the source that supported it is no longer present. The resulting change in inflow alters the system's ability to maintain continuity, regardless of how well the sequence was previously aligned or how predictable it was. The dependency structure defines the system's exposure to this type of failure.

The relationship between dependency and concentration also affects how the system responds to partial changes in sources. When a source is reduced rather than removed, the impact on the system depends on the degree of concentration. In a distributed structure, a reduction in one source produces a limited effect that can be absorbed by the remaining sources. In a concentrated structure, a reduction in the dominant source produces a significant change that affects the entire system. The system's response is therefore not only sensitive to the presence or absence of sources, but also to changes in their contribution.

This sensitivity extends to the system's ability to maintain continuity across time. When a dominant source is altered, the resulting change in inflow may disrupt the sequence of income, creating conditions similar to those described in earlier chapters. A reduction in inflow may introduce gaps or misalignment, even if the sequence was previously stable. The structural change in dependency therefore propagates into temporal instability. The loss of a source affects not only the amount of income, but also the behavior of income across time.

The connection between dependency and system behavior becomes clearer when considering how sources interact with the sequence of inflows. Each source contributes a portion of the sequence, and the overall pattern of income reflects the combined behavior of these sources. When one source dominates, the sequence is heavily influenced by its characteristics. When multiple sources contribute more evenly, the sequence reflects a combination of behaviors, reducing the influence of any single source. The structure of dependency therefore shapes the pattern of income over time.

The fragility introduced by concentration is often not immediately visible because it is embedded in the structure rather than in the observable behavior of income. A concentrated system may exhibit stable patterns and consistent inflows as long as the dominant source remains intact. The stability appears robust because the sequence behaves predictably. The underlying fragility is revealed only when the dependency is disrupted. At that point, the system's reliance on a single source becomes apparent, and the stability that appeared durable is exposed as conditional.

The apparent stability of a concentrated structure is therefore conditional rather than inherent. As long as the dominant source remains intact, the system can exhibit consistent inflows, predictable patterns, and alignment across time. These observable behaviors create the impression of durability. However, this stability is not generated by the structure itself. It is dependent on the continued existence of a specific condition within that structure. When that condition changes, the stability does not degrade gradually. It reconfigures abruptly because the system's primary support has been altered.

This conditional stability creates a distinction between systems that are robust and those that are merely intact. A distributed structure maintains continuity through the interaction of multiple sources, allowing the system to adjust to localized changes without altering its overall function. A concentrated structure does not possess this property. Its continuity is sustained by the persistence of a dominant dependency. When that dependency changes, the system does not redistribute load across other sources in a meaningful way. It transitions into a different operating state because the structure does not contain sufficient internal balance to absorb the change.

For this reason, fragility in a concentrated system is not an occasional outcome. It is an embedded characteristic. The system does not become fragile when the dominant source fails. It is already fragile, and the failure reveals that condition. Stability exists only within the boundary defined by the continuity of the dominant source. Once that boundary is crossed, the system's behavior changes in a way that reflects its underlying structure. The instability that follows is not introduced at the moment of failure. It is exposed by it.

The contrast between concentrated and distributed structures highlights the role of dependency in determining system resilience. In a distributed structure, the system can sustain the loss of individual sources without significant disruption to total income. The impact of each loss is limited, and the system retains a substantial portion of its inflow. In a concentrated structure, the system cannot sustain the loss of its dominant source without significant disruption. The impact of that loss is large, and the system must adjust to a new level of inflow that may be substantially lower than before.

This contrast establishes that stability depends on how dependency is distributed across sources. A system with evenly distributed dependency is less sensitive to changes in individual sources. A system with concentrated dependency is highly sensitive to changes in its dominant source. The distribution of dependency therefore determines the system's exposure to structural disruption. The same level of total income can produce different stability outcomes depending on how that income is generated.

The relationship between dependency and earlier forms of instability becomes evident when considering how the loss of a source affects sequence and continuity. The removal of a dominant source may create an immediate gap in the sequence of inflows, introducing absence where continuity previously existed. It may also alter the timing of remaining inflows, creating misalignment with obligations. In this way, dependency failure can trigger both sequence disruption and gaps, linking structural fragility to temporal instability. The initial cause is structural, but the effects propagate through the system's behavior over time.

This connection reinforces that stability must be evaluated across multiple dimensions. Time-based behavior, sequence alignment, and absence all influence how the system operates. Dependency structure defines the conditions under which these behaviors occur. When dependency is concentrated, the system is exposed to structural changes that can override prior stability. When dependency is distributed, the system is less exposed to such changes, and its behavior remains more consistent across time.

The defining characteristic of dependency risk is that it originates from the sources themselves. Income inherits its stability or instability from the structure of these sources. Concentration amplifies this inheritance by increasing the system's reliance on a small number of dependencies. The resulting fragility is not a function of how income behaves in isolation, but of how it is generated. Stability therefore depends on the distribution of dependency across sources, and fragility emerges when that distribution is narrow.

Skill Fragility

Income is generated through capability. Each inflow reflects the application of a specific set of abilities under particular conditions. These abilities define what types of income can be produced and under what circumstances that production remains viable. Capability therefore functions as a structural constraint on income. It determines not only the existence of inflow, but the range of possible inflows that the system can access. Income cannot extend beyond the boundaries defined by capability, because every source of income depends on the ability to produce value in a form that can be exchanged.

Earning capability can be understood as the structured set of functions through which income is created. This structure includes the range of tasks that can be performed, the conditions under which those tasks can be executed, and the contexts in which they are recognized as valuable. Capability is not a single attribute. It is a configuration of elements that together define what the system can do. This configuration establishes the limits of income generation. When capability is broad and adaptable, the system can produce income across a wider range of conditions. When capability is narrow, the system is constrained to a limited set of conditions.

The distinction between narrow and adaptable capability defines how the system responds to change. Narrow capability is characterized by dependence on specific conditions. It operates effectively within a defined context but does not extend easily beyond it. The applicability of such capability is limited, and its ability to generate income depends on the persistence of the conditions that support it. Adaptable capability, by contrast, is characterized by transferability across conditions. It can be applied in multiple contexts, allowing the system to produce income even when specific conditions change. The difference is not in the level of capability, but in its range of applicability.

This distinction introduces a form of internal dependency. Just as income depends on external sources, those sources depend on the system's capability to generate value. When capability is narrow, the system becomes dependent on the specific conditions that allow that capability to function. These conditions may include particular roles, environments, or forms of demand. The system's ability to produce income is therefore tied to the persistence of these conditions. When capability is adaptable, the system is less dependent on any single set of conditions. It can shift across contexts, maintaining its ability to generate income even as external conditions evolve.

Capability can therefore exhibit concentration similar to the concentration of income sources. When a large portion of income depends on a narrow set of capabilities, the system becomes internally concentrated. Its ability to generate income is tied to a limited range of functions. This concentration increases fragility because changes that affect the applicability of those functions have a disproportionate impact on the system. A system with broader capability distributes its income-generating potential across multiple functions, reducing sensitivity to changes in any one area.

The role of external demand introduces an additional layer of dependency. Capability produces income only when it is matched with demand. The presence of capability does not guarantee income generation. It must align with conditions in which its output is valued and exchanged. This alignment is determined by external factors that define whether a given capability is usable at a given time. When demand supports the capability, income is generated. When demand shifts, the same capability may no longer produce income in the same way. The system's stability is therefore influenced by how its capability structure interacts with changing conditions.

This interaction between capability and demand defines the usability of income-generating functions. A narrow capability that is closely aligned with current conditions may produce stable income as long as those conditions persist. The appearance of stability in this case is conditional. It depends on the continuation of a specific alignment between capability and demand. When conditions change, the usability of that capability can decline rapidly. An adaptable capability, by contrast, maintains usability across a wider range of conditions. Its alignment with demand is not limited to a single configuration, allowing it to sustain income generation even as external factors shift.

The mechanism through which capability influences stability is rooted in constraint and flexibility. Narrow capability constrains the system by limiting the number of contexts in which income can be generated. This limitation reduces the system's ability to adjust when conditions change. Adaptable capability introduces flexibility by expanding the range of contexts in which income can be produced. This flexibility increases the system's capacity to reconfigure its income generation in response to change. The difference between these two states determines how the system responds to disruptions in external conditions.

Behavior under stable conditions often obscures this distinction. When external conditions remain consistent, both narrow and adaptable capability can produce stable income. The system appears to function reliably because the alignment between capability and demand is maintained. In this state, the underlying structure of capability is not fully visible. The system's performance reflects the current conditions rather than its ability to adapt to new ones. Stability in this context is contingent on the persistence of those conditions, not on the inherent resilience of the capability structure.

When conditions begin to change, the difference between narrow and adaptable capability becomes apparent. Narrow capability, being dependent on specific conditions, loses viability as those conditions shift. The system's ability to generate income declines because the functions it relies on are no longer applicable in the same way. Adaptable capability, by contrast, can reconfigure its application to align with new conditions. The system maintains its ability to generate income by shifting across contexts. The divergence between these outcomes reflects the structural properties of capability rather than differences in magnitude or timing of income.

This divergence reveals a form of latent fragility within narrow capability structures. The system may appear stable while conditions remain favorable, but it contains an embedded dependency on those conditions. This dependency is not immediately visible because it does not affect the system's behavior under stable conditions. It becomes visible only when conditions change. At that point, the system's reliance on a narrow set of capabilities is exposed, and its ability to maintain income generation is reduced. The fragility is therefore latent, existing beneath the surface of apparent stability.

The limitation of narrow capability can be understood as a boundary rather than a gradient. Within a defined range of conditions, the system can produce income reliably because its capability aligns with what is required. Outside of that range, the system does not experience a gradual decline in effectiveness. It encounters a threshold beyond which the capability is no longer usable in a meaningful way. The transition from viable to non-viable occurs when conditions move beyond the scope of what the capability can support.

This boundary creates a discontinuity in the system's behavior. As long as conditions remain within the supported range, income generation appears stable and continuous. When conditions cross that boundary, the system's ability to generate income does not diminish incrementally. It breaks from one state to another because the underlying capability cannot extend into the new conditions. The system does not adapt within this transition because the structure of capability does not contain the necessary range.

For this reason, fragility in narrow capability is not defined by sensitivity alone, but by the presence of hard limits. The system remains stable only while conditions stay within those limits. When conditions move beyond them, the resulting instability is not a fluctuation in income but a loss of functionality. The capability does not produce less income. It ceases to produce income in that context. The instability that follows is therefore a direct consequence of the boundary embedded within the capability structure.

Failure in this context occurs when capability no longer matches the conditions required for income generation. The system's inflows decline or cease because the functions that previously produced income are no longer applicable. This failure does not require timing mismatch or extended gaps in the initial stage. It arises from a structural misalignment between capability and demand. The system may have operated with consistent timing and uninterrupted inflows prior to the change. The failure is triggered by a shift in conditions that renders the existing capability structure insufficient.

The absence of timing or sequence disruption in the initial phase of this failure distinguishes it from earlier forms of instability. The system does not fail because inflows arrive in the wrong order or because they are absent for a period. It fails because the mechanism that generates inflows is no longer functional under current conditions. The resulting decline in income may later produce gaps or misalignment, but the initial cause is structural. The system's capability no longer supports income generation in the existing environment.

The relationship between capability and dependency becomes clear when considering how sources of income are formed. Each source depends on the application of specific capabilities under certain conditions. The range of possible sources is therefore constrained by the capability structure. A narrow capability limits the number of viable sources, increasing dependency on a small set of conditions. An adaptable capability expands the range of possible sources, reducing dependency on any one set of conditions. The structure of capability thus determines the structure of dependency.

This connection establishes that internal fragility precedes external fragility. The concentration of dependency observed at the level of income sources originates in the concentration of capability. When capability is narrow, the system can access only a limited set of sources, leading to concentrated dependency. When capability is adaptable, the system can access a broader set of sources, allowing dependency to be more distributed. The external structure of income reflects the internal structure of capability.

The sensitivity of the system to change is therefore determined by how capability is configured. A narrow configuration creates high sensitivity because changes in conditions directly affect the system's ability to generate income. An adaptable configuration reduces sensitivity by allowing the system to shift its functions in response to change. This does not eliminate dependency on external conditions, but it reduces the system's reliance on any single configuration of those conditions. The system becomes more capable of maintaining continuity across different environments.

The presence of adaptable capability does not guarantee stability, but it alters the system's response to disruption. When conditions change, the system retains the ability to generate income through alternative applications of its capability. This retention supports continuity by providing pathways for income generation even as specific sources become unavailable. A narrow capability lacks this flexibility, resulting in a more abrupt decline in income when conditions shift. The system's response is therefore determined by the range of its capability rather than by the magnitude of its prior income.

The structural nature of this fragility means that it is not immediately visible in the behavior of income alone. A system with narrow capability may exhibit stable and predictable income as long as conditions remain favorable. The fragility exists beneath this stability, embedded in the system's limited ability to adapt. When conditions change, the transition from stability to instability can occur rapidly because the system lacks alternative pathways for income generation. The appearance of stability does not reflect the system's resilience to change, but its current alignment with conditions.

The evaluation of income stability must therefore include the structure of earning capability. Income cannot be understood solely through its observed behavior or its dependency on external sources. It must also be understood through the internal structure that makes those sources possible. Capability defines the boundaries within which income can be generated and the conditions under which it remains viable. The adaptability of this capability determines whether the system can maintain continuity when conditions change.

The relationship between capability, dependency, and income behavior establishes a hierarchy of constraints within the system. Capability constrains the range of possible sources. Sources determine the structure of income inflows. The behavior of those inflows defines how the system operates across time. When capability is narrow, the constraints at the top of this hierarchy are tight, limiting the system's flexibility at every level. When capability is adaptable, the constraints are broader, allowing greater flexibility in how income is generated and sustained.

Stability, in this context, depends on the adaptability of capability rather than on the stability of any specific source. A system with adaptable capability can maintain continuity across changing conditions because it can reconfigure its income generation. A system with narrow capability cannot. Its stability is tied to the persistence of specific conditions, and when those conditions change, the system's ability to generate income is reduced. The fragility of income is therefore rooted in the structure of capability, and stability emerges from the capacity of that structure to adapt across time.

External vs Internal Drivers

Income stability is shaped by forces that originate both within and outside the household financial system. Some of these forces arise from the structure of the system itself. Others are imposed on the system by conditions it does not determine. The distinction between these domains is central because it defines the boundary between what belongs to the system and what acts upon it. Stability cannot be explained by examining only one side of this boundary. It emerges from the interaction between internal capacity and external conditions.

Internal drivers originate within the system. They include the capability through which income can be generated and the structure through which effort is translated into output. These drivers define what the system can do. They establish the range of possible income-producing activity and the forms in which that activity can occur. Internal drivers do not guarantee income, but they determine the system's potential to produce it. They represent the productive structure of the system rather than the conditions under which that structure is recognized or rewarded.

External drivers originate outside the system. They include demand, the viability of income sources, and the surrounding conditions that determine whether internal capability can actually produce inflow. These drivers do not alter what the system is capable of doing in a direct structural sense. Instead, they determine whether that capability has a usable outlet. External drivers therefore govern the translation of potential into realized income. A system may retain its full internal structure while producing less income if external conditions no longer support the use of that structure.

The distinction is not between strength and weakness, but between origin and control. Internal drivers belong to the system because they are embedded in its structure. External drivers belong to the surrounding environment because they are imposed upon the system. Income stability is shaped by both. Internal drivers define productive capacity. External drivers define whether that capacity can be converted into inflow. Stability depends not on either domain in isolation, but on how closely they remain aligned across time.

Internal drivers establish the system's productive range. Capability defines what kinds of income can be generated and the conditions under which that generation remains possible. The structure of effort and output determines how the system converts its internal functions into external value. Together, these elements define the boundaries of potential. A system with broader internal capacity can operate across a wider set of conditions than a system whose productive structure is narrow. This broader range does not eliminate dependence on external conditions, but it changes the terms on which that dependence operates.

The significance of internal drivers lies in their role as conditions of possibility. They do not determine outcomes independently, but they determine which outcomes are even available to the system. Without sufficient capability, no external condition can produce income on behalf of the system. Internal structure is therefore necessary, but it is not sufficient. It defines what the system can do, not whether doing it will generate stable inflow. The existence of capability establishes potential. The realization of that potential depends on forces outside the system.

External drivers determine whether internal capacity is usable. Demand governs whether what the system can produce is valued in the current environment. Source availability determines whether channels exist through which that value can be exchanged for income. Broader conditions shape whether these channels remain stable or contract. External drivers therefore act as gate conditions. They do not create the system's capability, but they decide whether that capability is operative. Income is produced only when internal structure and external conditions intersect in a usable way.

This relationship defines the control boundary within the income system. Internal drivers are controllable only in a limited structural sense because they belong to the system itself. External drivers are not controllable because they originate outside it. The distinction is not absolute mastery on one side and total passivity on the other. It is a boundary of influence. Internal structure can be shaped by the system to some degree because it is endogenous. External conditions cannot be shaped in the same way because they are exogenous. Stability therefore depends on how exposed the system is to forces beyond this boundary.

Exposure measures the degree to which outcomes depend on what the system cannot determine. When external drivers dominate the conversion of capability into income, the system becomes more exposed. Its internal structure may remain intact, yet its realized income can change substantially because the governing conditions are outside the control boundary. Exposure does not imply immediate instability, but it defines the extent to which stability is contingent on the persistence of favorable conditions. The more a system relies on external continuity, the less its stability can be attributed to internal structure alone.

The interaction between control and exposure is central to understanding why internal strength does not eliminate external risk. A system may possess substantial capability and a coherent internal structure, yet still experience instability if demand shifts, conditions change, or source viability declines. The internal state of the system may be unchanged, but the outcome changes because external drivers have moved. This creates a structural asymmetry. Internal capacity is necessary for income generation, but it does not guarantee realized continuity when external conditions are unstable.

This asymmetry is often obscured during periods of stable external conditions. When demand is steady, sources remain viable, and surrounding conditions are supportive, the distinction between internal and external drivers becomes less visible. Income appears to follow naturally from internal capability, and stability is often attributed to the system itself. In reality, that stability may depend as much on external continuity as on internal structure. Because the external environment is not changing, its role fades from view. The system appears self-sustaining when it is actually operating within a favorable external field.

This creates a recurring misinterpretation. Stability is frequently attributed to internal factors because those factors are easier to observe from within the system. Capability, effort, and output appear to explain income because they are proximate and identifiable. External conditions appear passive because they are stable. The result is that stable outcomes are often read as evidence of internal control when they may instead reflect the temporary alignment of internal structure with supportive external conditions. Perceived control exceeds actual control because the external contribution to stability is not being actively registered.

The misinterpretation becomes more serious when stable outcomes persist long enough to seem inherent. The system then treats continuity as though it were produced primarily by internal drivers, even though external conditions may be doing much of the stabilizing work. The underlying exposure remains present but unobserved. As long as conditions do not change, the system can maintain the belief that stability is internally secured. The shift occurs only when external conditions begin to move. At that point, the distinction between internal structure and external support becomes visible.

Behavior under changing conditions reveals the true relationship between these domains. When external conditions shift, the system may retain the same capability and productive structure while experiencing different income outcomes. What changes is not the system itself, but the environment in which it operates. This divergence shows that income stability is not simply an expression of internal design. It is a negotiated outcome between what the system can do and whether external conditions permit that capability to produce income in a usable form.

The revealing function of change is important because exposure is often latent. It does not announce itself during stable periods. It becomes visible only when the environment begins to place pressure on the system. A capability that seemed fully sufficient under one set of conditions may become partially or wholly unusable under another. Source structures that appeared durable may weaken or disappear. Demand that once translated capability into income may contract. The system then encounters a form of instability that does not originate from internal degradation. It originates from the movement of external drivers.

This means that failure can occur without any internal change. The system may preserve the same capability, effort structure, and productive coherence, yet still experience a decline in income if external conditions shift beyond what that capability can support. Failure in this sense is not a breakdown of internal function. It is a breakdown in the alignment between internal function and external reality. The system remains what it was, but the conditions that made its income possible no longer hold. The result is an externally driven failure state.

The significance of this failure mode lies in its independence from internal decline. It demonstrates that capability alone cannot secure stability if the surrounding conditions that validate or support that capability are unstable. The system may be internally unchanged and still become unstable because the decisive variable moved outside it. This clarifies why internal control has structural limits. The system can define its own capacity, but it cannot define the environment in which that capacity must operate. Stability therefore depends not on internal structure alone, but on the continued compatibility between internal and external domains.

The relationship to earlier chapters becomes clearer within this framework. Dependency, previously examined through the structure of sources, belongs primarily to the domain of external exposure. Sources exist outside the system and determine whether inflows continue. Capability, previously examined as a constraint on earning potential, belongs primarily to the domain of internal structure. It defines what kinds of sources are even accessible to the system. These are not separate explanations of stability. They are interacting layers. Internal capability shapes the range of possible dependencies, while external conditions determine whether those dependencies remain viable.

This interaction means that neither domain can be understood independently. Internal capability without viable external conditions remains unrealized. External demand without corresponding internal capability remains inaccessible. Income emerges only where these domains intersect. Stability depends on whether that intersection can be maintained over time. If internal capability is narrow, the system is more exposed because fewer external alignments can sustain it. If external conditions become unstable, even broad capability may produce weaker continuity if the available channels of conversion contract. The system is always operating within both domains at once.

The control boundary clarifies the origin of fragility. Fragility arises not merely from weakness within the system, but from the extent to which outcomes depend on conditions beyond the system. A system may be internally coherent yet externally exposed. In such a case, apparent stability is conditional rather than secured. The controlling structure exists inside the system, but the decisive pressures may come from outside it. The greater this asymmetry, the more unstable the system becomes under environmental change.

This is why stability cannot be accurately described as something the system simply possesses. It is not a fixed internal attribute. It is a contingent state produced by alignment between internal capacity and external conditions. Internal drivers define the system's productive possibilities. External drivers define whether those possibilities convert into realized income. The resulting stability is therefore neither wholly internal nor wholly external. It is relational. It exists only as long as the system's internal structure remains compatible with the conditions imposed upon it.

The distinction between what can be influenced and what cannot be controlled is therefore essential to interpreting income behavior. Internal structure can shape potential, range, and adaptability, but it cannot eliminate exposure to external movement. External drivers determine whether internal capacity produces stable inflow, and they do so without regard to the system's internal coherence. Stability emerges only where these domains remain aligned. When they diverge, fragility becomes visible.

Income stability is therefore not controlled in any complete sense. It is negotiated between internal capacity and external conditions, between what the system can produce and what the environment will support. The system may strengthen its internal structure, but its outcomes remain exposed to forces beyond that structure. Fragility comes from this exposure boundary. Stability persists only while the interaction between internal drivers and external forces remains intact.

Income Layering

Income does not operate as a uniform stream within a household financial system. It is composed of multiple inflows that differ in magnitude, timing, dependency, and responsiveness to change. These inflows can be organized into a structure in which each component serves a distinct role. Income layering refers to the structural differentiation of these inflows into functional categories that contribute to stability in different ways. Rather than treating all income as interchangeable, layering recognizes that different portions of income perform different tasks within the system.

The presence of multiple inflows does not, by itself, create a layered structure. Layering requires differentiation by function. Each component of income must be understood in terms of the role it plays rather than its size alone. This differentiation allows the system to allocate distinct responsibilities to different inflows, creating a structured arrangement rather than a collection of equivalent parts. The system then operates not as a single stream, but as a composite of layers, each with its own behavioral characteristics and contribution to continuity.

Within this structure, income can be divided into three primary functional layers. These layers are defined by their role within the system rather than by their absolute magnitude or perceived importance. The primary layer represents the main source of inflow, typically contributing the largest share of total income. The secondary layer consists of supporting inflows that supplement the primary source and reduce reliance on it. The supplemental layer includes smaller or more variable inflows that add flexibility to the system. These categories are not hierarchical in value. They are structural distinctions that describe how different inflows function within the system.

The primary layer provides the foundational component of income. It is characterized by its magnitude and its central role in sustaining the system's baseline operation. Because it contributes the largest share of inflow, it often defines the system's scale. This concentration of contribution also creates concentration of dependency. The system becomes structurally tied to the continuity of the primary layer, as a significant portion of its inflow depends on this single component. The primary layer stabilizes magnitude by providing a consistent base, but it simultaneously concentrates exposure by linking a large portion of the system's stability to one source.

The secondary layer functions as a supporting structure that reduces reliance on the primary layer. It introduces additional inflows that operate alongside the primary source, contributing to the system without dominating it. These inflows are typically smaller than the primary layer but are substantial enough to influence the system's behavior. By distributing a portion of income generation across additional sources, the secondary layer reduces the system's sensitivity to changes in the primary layer. It does not eliminate dependency, but it alters its distribution, making the system less reliant on a single component.

The supplemental layer operates at a smaller scale and with greater variability. It consists of inflows that are often irregular, intermittent, or responsive to changing conditions. These inflows do not define the system's baseline, nor do they significantly alter its scale. Instead, they provide flexibility. The supplemental layer allows the system to adjust to variation, absorb fluctuations, and respond to changes without requiring structural shifts in the primary or secondary layers. Its contribution is not measured primarily in magnitude, but in adaptability.

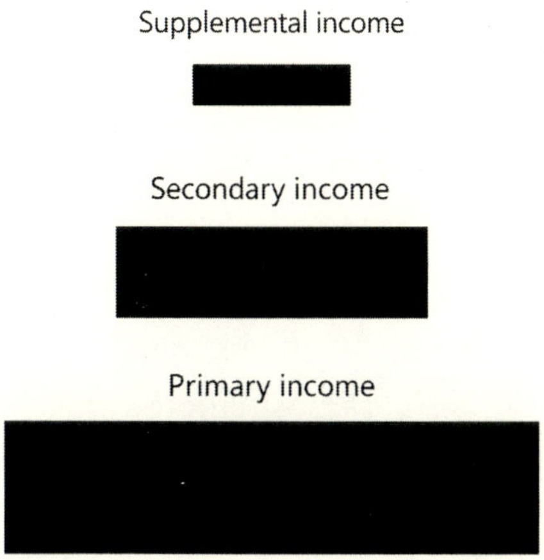

Figure 9 – Layered Stack

The differentiation of these layers changes how the system behaves. When income is treated as a single undifferentiated stream, all functions are imposed on that stream simultaneously. It must provide magnitude, absorb variation, and respond to change without structural separation. This creates tension within the system, as a single component is required to perform multiple roles that may not be compatible. In a layered structure, these roles are distributed. The primary layer stabilizes magnitude, the secondary layer moderates dependency, and the supplemental layer provides flexibility. Stability emerges not from the uniformity of income, but from the separation of these functions across layers.

This separation alters how the system absorbs instability. Different types of disruption affect different layers in different ways. A disruption that affects the primary layer has a large impact on magnitude but may be partially offset by the presence of secondary and supplemental layers. A disruption in the supplemental layer has a limited impact on total income but may reduce the system's flexibility. The layered structure ensures that no single disruption affects all functions simultaneously. Each layer absorbs or transmits instability according to its role, preventing the system from collapsing under a single point of stress.

The interaction between layers is central to this behavior. The layers are not independent components operating in isolation. They are interconnected parts of a single system. The primary layer provides the baseline that supports the system's core operation. The secondary layer adjusts the load on the primary layer by contributing additional inflows that reduce concentration. The supplemental layer absorbs variation by responding to changes that the other layers are not structured to handle. Together, these interactions create a dynamic system in which stability is maintained through the coordination of differentiated roles.

The presence of layering allows the system to distribute the impact of disruption across multiple components. In a single-layer system, any disruption affects the entire structure because there is no differentiation of roles. The system depends entirely on one component, and any change in that component translates directly into system-wide instability. In a layered system, disruption is localized. A change in one layer affects the system, but the presence of other layers provides a degree of separation that limits the propagation of that change. The system remains intact because its functions are not concentrated in a single element.

The effect of this distribution is not only a reduction in immediate impact, but a change in how disruption moves through the system.

In a single-layer structure, disruption propagates directly because there is no separation between functions. A reduction in inflow affects magnitude, flexibility, and continuity simultaneously, as all of these roles are concentrated within the same component. The system has no internal boundaries to contain the disruption, and the effect spreads without resistance across all aspects of its operation.

In a layered structure, propagation is mediated by the differentiation of roles. Each layer absorbs disruption according to its function, and the presence of adjacent layers introduces a form of structural buffering. A disturbance affecting the primary layer alters the system's scale, but the secondary and supplemental layers continue to operate within their own functional ranges. A disturbance affecting the supplemental layer reduces flexibility but does not directly compromise the system's baseline. The separation of roles creates partial isolation between functions, limiting the extent to which disruption in one layer transfers into others.

This mediation does not eliminate instability, but it changes its trajectory. Instead of producing an immediate system-wide effect, disruption becomes segmented. It is absorbed, redistributed, or contained within specific layers before it can affect the system as a whole. The system's response becomes staged rather than simultaneous. This staging allows continuity to be maintained even as individual components are affected, because the system's core functions are not fully exposed to a single point of disruption. The stability that emerges from layering is therefore not the absence of disturbance, but the presence of structure that limits how disturbance propagates.

This contrast highlights the role of layering in reducing fragility. A single-layer system is inherently concentrated. All income functions are tied to one source, creating high exposure to changes in that source. A layered system distributes these functions across multiple components, reducing concentration and spreading exposure. The system becomes less sensitive to changes in any one component because its stability does not depend entirely on that component. The reduction in fragility arises from this distribution of roles rather than from an increase in total income.

The absence of layering produces a structure in which income is both concentrated and undifferentiated. The system relies on a single stream to perform all functions, creating a condition where stability depends entirely on the continuity of that stream. This condition amplifies the effects of dependency, capability constraints, and external exposure. Any disruption in the single stream affects all aspects of the system simultaneously, leading to a rapid transition from stability to instability. The failure mode is therefore structural. It arises from the lack of differentiation within the income system.

Layering addresses this structural limitation by introducing internal organization. It does not eliminate external exposure or internal constraints, but it changes how these factors affect the system. By distributing functions across layers, the system reduces the extent to which any single factor can destabilize it. Dependency is spread across multiple components, capability is expressed through multiple pathways, and exposure to external conditions is mediated by the interaction of layers. The system becomes more resilient not because it avoids instability, but because it is structured to absorb and distribute it.

The relationship between layering and earlier concepts becomes evident when viewed through this structural lens. Dependency, previously associated with concentration of income sources, is moderated by the presence of secondary and supplemental layers. Capability, previously understood as a constraint on income generation, is expressed across multiple layers, reflecting a broader range of functions. External exposure, previously defined by the interaction between internal and external drivers, is reduced in its impact because no single layer carries the entire burden of that exposure. Layering integrates these elements into a coherent structure.

The stability of the system is therefore not determined by the magnitude of any single layer, but by the arrangement of layers and the roles they perform. A system with a large primary layer and no supporting layers remains fragile because its stability is concentrated. A system with multiple layers, even if the total income is unchanged, exhibits different behavior because its functions are distributed. The presence of layering changes the system's response to disruption, allowing it to maintain continuity across a wider range of conditions.

The effect of layering extends beyond the immediate absorption of disruption and into how the system behaves across time. In a single-layer structure, any change in conditions forces the entire system to adjust simultaneously because all functions are concentrated within one component. The system cannot reallocate responsibility or shift load between parts. As conditions evolve, the system must either maintain alignment in its existing form or experience a direct breakdown in continuity. There is no internal mechanism through which gradual adjustment can occur.

In a layered structure, adjustment becomes possible through reconfiguration rather than collapse. Because functions are separated across layers, changes in conditions can be absorbed unevenly, allowing the system to shift how income is generated and supported over time. A reduction in the primary layer may increase the relative importance of secondary inflows. Variability in the supplemental layer may be absorbed without altering the system's baseline. The system does not rely on a single configuration to remain viable. It can transition between configurations while maintaining continuity.

This capacity for reconfiguration introduces a form of temporal flexibility. Stability is no longer dependent on maintaining a fixed structure under changing conditions. Instead, it emerges from the system's ability to adjust the balance between layers as those conditions evolve. The system remains continuous not because it resists change, but because it can redistribute function across its internal structure without losing coherence. Layering therefore transforms stability from a static condition into a dynamic process that unfolds across time.

This structural approach reframes income from a quantity to a system design. The question is not how much income exists, but how that income is organized. Each layer contributes to stability in a different way, and the interaction between layers defines the system's behavior. Stability emerges from this interaction, not from the properties of any individual component. The layered structure provides a framework through which income can be understood as a coordinated system rather than as a single stream.

The defining insight of layering is that not all income should perform the same function within the system. When roles are differentiated, the system can allocate stability, flexibility, and support across distinct components. This allocation reduces the burden on any single layer and allows the system to absorb variation without losing continuity. The structure itself becomes the mechanism through which stability is achieved.

Redundancy Without Overload

Income layering introduces structure by assigning differentiated roles to multiple inflows within a system. That structure implies redundancy. Redundancy exists when the system is not dependent on a single pathway for income generation, but instead operates through multiple pathways that can sustain continuity if one component changes. Redundancy distributes risk by ensuring that the system's stability does not depend entirely on any one element. It creates alternative routes through which income can continue to flow, reducing the likelihood that a single disruption will produce system-wide failure.

Redundancy is therefore a structural property rather than a numerical one. It is not defined by the presence of multiple inflows alone, but by the extent to which those inflows function as independent pathways capable of sustaining the system under changing conditions. When redundancy is present, the system can absorb disruptions because its capacity is not concentrated in a single component. When redundancy is absent, the system becomes dependent on a single pathway, and its stability is contingent on the uninterrupted function of that pathway. The introduction of redundancy addresses this dependency by distributing the system's exposure across multiple components.

The necessity of redundancy arises from the limitations of single-path systems. When income is concentrated in a single pathway, the system inherits the full set of risks associated with that pathway. Any change in its conditions directly affects the entire system. There is no separation between component-level disruption and system-level outcome. The system either continues or fails in direct correspondence with the state of that single pathway. This creates a form of fragility that is structural rather than situational. Stability cannot be maintained unless the pathway itself remains uninterrupted.

Introducing redundancy changes this relationship by decoupling system continuity from any one component. Multiple pathways allow the system to maintain operation even when one pathway is altered or removed. The system's response to disruption becomes distributed rather than concentrated. A change in one component produces a partial effect rather than a complete one. This partial effect can be absorbed within the structure, allowing the system to continue functioning. Redundancy therefore acts as a stabilizing mechanism by reducing the system's sensitivity to individual disruptions.

However, the presence of redundancy does not imply that more redundancy always improves stability. The introduction of additional pathways increases the number of components within the system. Each component requires coordination, integration, and maintenance. As the number of components grows, the system becomes more complex. This complexity introduces a different form of fragility, one that arises not from concentration but from the burden of managing multiple interacting elements. Redundancy reduces one type of risk while introducing another.

Insufficient redundancy defines the lower boundary of the system. When redundancy is too low, the system remains highly concentrated. A small number of pathways carry a large share of the system's income, creating high sensitivity to disruption. The system's behavior under stress reflects this concentration. Changes in one component produce large effects because there are no alternative pathways to offset them. The system is exposed to abrupt instability, where continuity can be lost quickly if a primary pathway is disrupted. This condition reflects under-structuring rather than over-structuring.

Excess redundancy defines the upper boundary. When the number of pathways increases beyond a certain point, the system begins to experience fragmentation. Each additional component introduces its own conditions, timing, and requirements for coordination. The system must manage these components simultaneously, integrating their behavior into a coherent structure. As the number of components grows, the effort required to maintain this coherence increases. The system becomes more difficult to manage, and the relationships between components become more complex.

This complexity introduces structural overhead. Overhead represents the resources required to coordinate and maintain the system's components rather than to generate income directly. As redundancy increases, overhead grows because more components must be managed. Each pathway requires attention, alignment with other pathways, and integration into the system's overall operation. The system must track multiple inflows, each with its own behavior and constraints. The cumulative effect is an increase in the burden placed on the system to sustain its own structure.

The introduction of additional components also creates more points of potential failure. Each pathway has its own dependencies, conditions, and sources of variability. As the number of pathways increases, the number of these points increases as well. The system becomes more exposed to internal coordination failure, where the interaction between components becomes unstable. This form of fragility is distinct from the fragility of concentration. It arises from the complexity of the system itself rather than from its reliance on any single component.

The relationship between redundancy and stability is therefore non-linear. Initial increases in redundancy produce significant improvements in stability by reducing concentration and distributing risk. As redundancy continues to increase, the marginal benefit of each additional pathway declines. The system gains less additional stability from each new component while incurring greater complexity costs. This creates a condition of diminishing returns, where the balance between benefit and cost shifts as the system becomes more complex.

The progression toward excess redundancy often occurs without explicit recognition because the initial benefits of diversification are clear while the costs of complexity accumulate gradually. Early additions of new pathways produce visible improvements in stability by reducing concentration and distributing risk. These improvements reinforce further expansion, creating a tendency to continue adding components under the assumption that the same benefits will persist. However, the structural conditions that made early additions effective do not scale linearly. As the system grows, each additional pathway contributes less to stability while increasing the burden of coordination.

This asymmetry between visible benefit and deferred cost creates a directional bias within the system. The system is incentivized to expand redundancy because the initial gains are immediate and observable, while the costs of complexity emerge slowly through increased coordination demands and reduced coherence. The result is a gradual transition from beneficial redundancy to structural overload without a clear boundary marking the shift. The system does not experience a discrete change, but a progressive accumulation of complexity that eventually alters its behavior.

At this point, additional redundancy no longer contributes meaningfully to stability. Instead, it begins to introduce instability through increased complexity. The system must manage a larger number of interactions, each with its own potential for misalignment. Coordination becomes more difficult, and the system's ability to function as a unified structure begins to weaken. The presence of multiple pathways no longer provides clear stabilization because the interactions between those pathways become a source of instability in themselves.

System overload occurs when complexity exceeds the system's capacity to maintain coherence. In this condition, the structure becomes fragmented. The system is composed of many components, but those components no longer operate as an integrated whole. Coordination breaks down, and the reliability of individual pathways becomes inconsistent. The system may still contain multiple sources of income, but its ability to manage them effectively is diminished. Stability is compromised not by a lack of redundancy, but by the inability to sustain the structure created by that redundancy.

The characteristics of overload reflect this fragmentation. The system experiences difficulty maintaining alignment across its components. Interactions between pathways become unstable, and the system's behavior becomes less predictable. The presence of multiple pathways does not translate into effective redundancy because the system cannot coordinate them into a coherent structure. Instead, the complexity of the system becomes a source of instability, offsetting the benefits that redundancy was intended to provide.

The trade-off between redundancy and complexity defines the system's operating range. Stability exists within a bounded region where redundancy is sufficient to reduce concentration but not so extensive that it creates overload. This region is not defined by a fixed number of pathways, but by the relationship between the number of components and the system's capacity to integrate them. The system must maintain coherence while distributing risk. When either of these conditions is violated, stability declines.

At the lower boundary, insufficient redundancy leads to concentration and high sensitivity to disruption. The system fails quickly when a primary pathway is altered because there are no alternative pathways to sustain continuity. At the upper boundary, excessive redundancy leads to fragmentation and coordination failure. The system degrades gradually as complexity undermines its ability to function as a unified whole. These failure modes differ in form, but both represent departures from the balanced region where stability is maximized.

The distinction between these failure modes highlights the importance of system coherence. Coherence refers to the system's ability to operate as an integrated structure rather than as a collection of independent components. A coherent system maintains alignment across its pathways, allowing them to function together in a coordinated manner. When coherence is lost, the system's components may still exist, but their interactions become unstable. The system no longer behaves predictably, and its capacity to maintain continuity is reduced.

Redundancy interacts with coherence in a fundamental way. As redundancy increases, the potential for distributing risk improves, but the challenge of maintaining coherence also increases. The system must balance these effects. Too little redundancy preserves coherence but concentrates risk. Too much redundancy distributes risk but undermines coherence. Stability depends on maintaining both, which requires that redundancy remain within the system's capacity to manage it.

The relationship between redundancy and prior structural elements reinforces this balance. Redundancy reduces dependency concentration by distributing income across multiple pathways. It reflects the range of capability by enabling multiple forms of income generation. It interacts with external exposure by reducing reliance on any single set of conditions. At the same time, redundancy introduces complexity, which must be integrated into the system's overall structure. The effectiveness of redundancy depends on how well it is incorporated into a coherent system.

The resulting framework defines stability as a function of balanced structure. Stability is not achieved by minimizing redundancy, nor by maximizing it. It is achieved by maintaining sufficient redundancy to distribute risk while preserving the system's ability to operate as a unified whole. This balance reflects the system's constraints. There is no configuration that eliminates all risk or all complexity. The system must operate within a range where both are managed.

The central implication is that every structural improvement carries a corresponding cost. Redundancy improves stability by reducing concentration, but it increases complexity. Complexity introduces new forms of fragility that must be accounted for. The system cannot eliminate this trade-off. It can only position itself within it. Stability emerges from this positioning, where the benefits of redundancy are realized without exceeding the system's capacity to sustain its structure.

The boundary between stability and instability is therefore defined by the interaction of these forces. A system that is too simple is exposed to concentrated risk. A system that is too complex is exposed to coordination failure. Between these extremes lies a region where redundancy and coherence are balanced. Within this region, the system can absorb disruption without becoming fragmented. Outside it, stability declines for different reasons at each boundary.

Income stability, in this context, is not a function of increasing the number of income components indefinitely. It is a function of structuring those components within the limits of the system's capacity. Redundancy must be sufficient to distribute risk, but not so extensive that it overwhelms the system's ability to integrate its parts. Stability is achieved through this balance, where the system remains both diversified and coherent.

Smoothing Income

Income systems do not operate in an environment of unlimited flexibility. Structural arrangements, once established, exist within boundaries that restrict how they can be modified, expanded, or simplified. Constraint defines these boundaries. It represents the limits placed on a system's ability to adjust its structure, reallocate its components, or respond to changing conditions. These limits are not temporary conditions but persistent characteristics of the system's operating environment. As a result, income stability cannot be understood solely through structural design. It must be understood through how that structure behaves when adjustment is restricted.

Constraint alters the nature of system behavior by reducing flexibility. In an unconstrained framework, structural elements such as layering or redundancy can be modified to address emerging instability. Additional components can be introduced, existing components can be removed, and roles can be redefined. Under constraint, these adjustments become difficult. The system cannot easily add new layers to reduce dependency, nor can it simplify existing structures to reduce complexity. The range of possible changes narrows, and the system must function within the configuration that already exists. Flexibility transitions from an assumed property to a limited resource.

This reduction in flexibility leads to a condition in which prior structural decisions become fixed. Choices that were previously adjustable become embedded within the system. The distribution of income across layers, the degree of redundancy, and the complexity of coordination are no longer variables that can be readily altered. Instead, they define the system's operating state. Trade-offs that were initially selected as part of the system's design become constraints on its future behavior. The system must operate with these trade-offs rather than revisiting them.

Constraint does not act on individual components in isolation. It propagates through the system by linking limitations across multiple dimensions. A restriction in one area reduces flexibility in others, creating a cascading effect. When the system cannot adjust its layering, it also cannot easily redistribute dependency. When redundancy cannot be modified, exposure to disruption remains fixed. The system's limitations become interconnected, and constraint in one dimension reinforces constraint in another.

This interconnectedness changes how the system responds to pressure. Adjustments that might resolve instability in one part of the system cannot be implemented because they require changes in another part that is also constrained. The system becomes internally coupled, with each limitation reinforcing the persistence of others. Constraint therefore operates not as a single boundary, but as a network of boundaries that restrict the system's ability to reorganize itself.

Capacity limits reinforce this condition. Every system has a finite ability to manage components, coordinate interactions, and sustain complexity. This capacity is not expandable without cost. It is bounded by factors such as time, attention, and the ability to maintain alignment across components. When the system approaches these limits, its ability to incorporate additional elements or to reorganize existing ones diminishes. The complexity ceiling established in earlier structural considerations becomes a binding constraint. The system cannot exceed it without introducing instability.

Adaptation under these conditions becomes a process characterized by friction. Change requires effort, and effort is limited. Adjustments that might appear straightforward in an unconstrained context require time, coordination, and reallocation of resources. The system cannot transition instantly from one configuration to another. Instead, it must navigate the process of change within its existing limitations. This friction slows adaptation and introduces delays between the recognition of instability and the implementation of structural adjustments.

Constraint also alters the system's relationship with time. In an unconstrained system, adjustment can occur relatively quickly in response to changing conditions. Under constraint, the timeline of response extends. Delays accumulate between the onset of instability, the recognition of that instability, and the system's ability to respond. These delays create a gap between conditions and adjustment, during which the system continues to operate in a misaligned state.

This temporal distortion amplifies the effects of instability. Because the system cannot adjust immediately, small imbalances persist longer and interact with other components. What might have been a localized disruption becomes more significant as it propagates through the system over time. The system's behavior is therefore shaped not only by the presence of constraint, but by the delay it introduces into the adjustment process.

The presence of constraint forces prioritization. A system cannot optimize all dimensions simultaneously when its capacity to adjust is limited. Trade-offs that were previously theoretical become operational realities. Increasing redundancy may not be feasible if it exceeds the system's capacity for coordination. Reducing complexity may not be possible if existing components are interdependent. The system must allocate its limited capacity to certain dimensions while accepting limitations in others. Stability is therefore influenced not only by structural design but by how the system prioritizes within its constraints.

Constraint also compresses the system's decision space. In an unconstrained environment, multiple adjustment paths may be available, allowing the system to choose between alternative configurations. Under constraint, these alternatives narrow. The system is not selecting from a wide range of options, but from a limited set of feasible actions. Some adjustments are no longer possible because they exceed the system's capacity, require changes that cannot be implemented, or conflict with existing structural commitments.

This compression alters the nature of decision-making. Choices are no longer evaluated based on optimal outcomes, but on what can be executed within the system's limits. The system may recognize a more stable configuration, yet be unable to move toward it because the transition exceeds its available capacity or disrupts existing dependencies. Decisions become constrained not by preference, but by feasibility. The system operates within a reduced decision space where the range of viable actions is bounded by its structure and its limits.

The result is that stability is often maintained through constrained decisions rather than optimal ones. The system selects actions that preserve continuity within its limitations, even if those actions do not represent the most efficient or stable configuration in an abstract sense. This reinforces the distinction between ideal structure and operational reality. Under constraint, the system does not move toward the best possible state. It moves toward the best state that remains reachable.

Under pressure, constrained systems exhibit distinct patterns of behavior. They do not typically transition immediately from stability to failure. Instead, they undergo gradual changes in state. Components may become less reliable, coordination may weaken, and the system may begin to operate with reduced efficiency. Resources are reallocated to maintain critical functions, while less essential functions are compressed or deferred. This process reflects the system's attempt to maintain continuity within its constraints. Failure, when it occurs, is often the result of accumulated strain rather than a single event.

Under constraint, failure does not typically emerge as a discrete break from one state to another. Instead, it develops through the gradual accumulation of unresolved pressures within the system. Because adjustments are limited, imbalances are not corrected as they arise. They persist and interact, creating layers of strain that build over time. The system continues to function, but with increasing inefficiency and reduced reliability.

This accumulation produces a distinct failure pattern. Rather than collapsing immediately, the system degrades. Components become less coordinated, responses become slower, and the ability to maintain continuity weakens incrementally. The transition from stability to instability is therefore extended, with multiple intermediate states rather than a single point of failure. Constraint shapes this progression by preventing the system from resetting or reorganizing before the accumulated strain becomes significant.

Constraint also affects the system's ability to recover once instability has developed. In an unconstrained environment, recovery can occur through reconfiguration. The system can reduce complexity, redistribute dependency, or introduce new pathways to restore balance. Under constraint, these recovery mechanisms are limited. The same boundaries that restrict initial adjustment also restrict the system's ability to reverse degradation.

This creates a condition in which recovery is asymmetrical relative to decline. Degradation can accumulate gradually through the interaction of unresolved pressures, but recovery requires coordinated change across multiple components. Because these changes are constrained, the system cannot easily retrace its path back to a prior state. Instead, it must stabilize within its altered structure, often at a lower level of efficiency or reliability.

The effort required for recovery therefore exceeds the effort required for decline. Degradation emerges from the passive accumulation of imbalance, while recovery requires active reorganization within limited capacity. The system must allocate resources to rebuild coordination, restore reliability, and reestablish alignment across components, all while continuing to operate. This creates tension between maintaining current function and investing in structural repair.

As a result, constrained systems often exhibit partial recovery rather than full restoration. Stability may be reestablished, but not in the same configuration or at the same level as before. The system adapts to its new state rather than returning to its previous one. Recovery becomes a process of re-stabilization within constraint rather than a return to an unconstrained baseline.

Constraint also introduces path dependence into the system's behavior. The current structure is the result of prior decisions, and these decisions limit the range of future options. The system cannot reset to an ideal configuration without incurring significant cost or disruption. Instead, it must evolve from its existing state. This creates a dependency on historical structure. The system's ability to respond to new conditions is shaped by the choices that were made under previous conditions. Path dependence reinforces the persistence of structure, even when that structure is no longer optimal.

Within this context, stability is redefined. It is no longer a condition that can be maximized through structural adjustment. It becomes a condition that must be maintained within the limits imposed by constraint. The system cannot eliminate instability entirely, nor can it fully optimize its structure. Instead, it operates within a bounded range where stability is preserved to the extent possible. This preservation requires managing the interaction between existing structure and current conditions rather than redesigning the system.

The influence of constraint extends across all previously defined dimensions of income stability. Dependency structures cannot be easily redistributed when constraint limits the ability to introduce or remove components. Capability cannot be expanded immediately when adaptation requires time and effort. External drivers continue to affect the system regardless of its internal configuration, and the system's ability to respond to these drivers is limited by its constraints. Layering, once established, becomes a fixed arrangement rather than a flexible tool. Redundancy, once balanced, cannot be adjusted freely without affecting system coherence.

These interactions reinforce the central role of constraint in determining system behavior. The system's design provides a framework, but constraint governs how that framework operates in practice. The distinction between ideal structure and actual operation becomes apparent. An ideal structure assumes the ability to adjust components as needed. Actual operation reflects the limits on that ability. The system must function within these limits, and its stability depends on how effectively it does so.

The bounded nature of the system creates a condition in which trade-offs are unavoidable. Every adjustment involves a cost, and every decision must be made within the system's capacity. The system cannot pursue all improvements simultaneously, nor can it eliminate all sources of instability. It must accept certain limitations while managing others. Stability emerges from this process of operating within constraint rather than from achieving an optimal configuration.

The persistence of structure under constraint also shapes how instability develops. Because the system cannot be easily reconfigured, imbalances may persist over time. Dependency concentrations may remain in place, complexity may remain elevated, and capacity limits may continue to bind. The system must absorb these conditions rather than resolve them immediately. This absorption process defines the system's resilience. It reflects the ability to maintain function despite the presence of unresolved structural tensions.

Constraint therefore shifts the focus from design to operation. The question is no longer how the system should be structured in an ideal sense, but how it behaves given the structure it has and the limits it faces.

Stability is not a property that can be engineered once and maintained indefinitely. It is a condition that must be sustained within the system's constraints. The system's behavior under these constraints determines whether stability can be preserved.

The resulting framework positions constraint as the governing factor in income stability. Structural elements such as layering and redundancy define the system's potential, but constraint defines its actual performance. The system cannot exceed its limits, and its ability to adapt is bounded. Stability is achieved not by eliminating these limits, but by operating effectively within them.

Income Shock

Income systems operate on the assumption of continuity. Inflows are expected to arrive with sufficient regularity and reliability to sustain the structure that depends on them. This expectation does not require perfect consistency, but it does require that deviations remain within a range that preserves system function. Income shock represents the point at which this expectation is violated. It is not a variation within the flow, nor a fluctuation that can be absorbed through normal system behavior. It is a break in continuity, where expected inflow fails to occur in the manner required to sustain the system.

A shock is therefore defined as an interruption of expected inflow. It is distinguished from variability by its structural impact. Variability occurs within the boundaries of expectation, even when it introduces uncertainty. Shock exists outside those boundaries. It alters the conditions under which the system operates by removing or degrading the inflow that the system depends on. This distinction is essential because it separates normal system behavior from destabilizing events. A system can function under variability, but it must respond differently when continuity itself is disrupted.

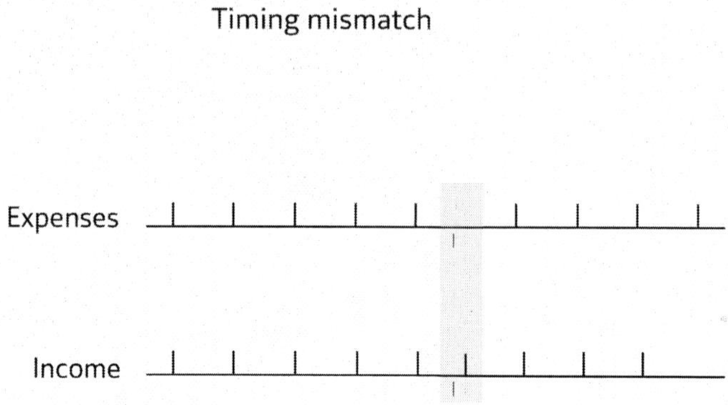

Figure 10 – Interruption Timeline

Continuity forms the baseline condition for system stability. The structure of income, including its layering and distribution, assumes that inflows will persist over time. This persistence allows the system to maintain alignment between inflows and obligations, to distribute load across layers, and to operate within its established constraints. Stability emerges from this ongoing flow rather than from the total amount of income accumulated. When continuity is maintained, the system can function even with variability. When continuity is broken, the system must transition to a different state.

Shock enters the system as an interruption event. This interruption can take multiple forms, but its defining characteristic is the disruption of expected inflow. The interruption may be partial, where inflow is reduced but not eliminated. It may be total, where inflow ceases entirely. It may be temporary, where the interruption is limited in duration, or permanent, where the inflow does not return. Regardless of its form, the interruption represents the initial point at which the system deviates from its expected behavior. It is the starting condition from which instability may develop, but it does not in itself constitute system failure.

The nature of the interruption determines how the system perceives and responds to the shock. A fundamental distinction exists between sudden and gradual shocks. A sudden shock occurs as an immediate and discrete event. It produces a visible break in continuity, where inflow that was expected at a specific point in time fails to occur. The system experiences an abrupt change in state, with little or no time to adjust. The impact is immediate because the absence of inflow is directly observable at the moment it occurs.

In contrast, a gradual shock unfolds over time. It is characterized by a progressive degradation of inflow rather than a single point of interruption. The system continues to receive income, but the pattern of that income changes in a way that reduces its effectiveness. The change may be in magnitude, timing, or reliability, but it occurs incrementally. Because the flow does not cease entirely, the system may interpret the change as variability rather than as a structural break. The visibility of the shock is therefore reduced, and its impact accumulates over time rather than appearing instantly.

This difference in visibility leads to a difference in detection. Sudden shocks are identified quickly because they produce an immediate deviation from expectation. The system recognizes the absence of inflow as a break in continuity and responds accordingly. Gradual shocks are more difficult to detect because they resemble normal variation in their early stages. The system may continue to operate under the assumption of continuity, even as the underlying conditions deteriorate. This delay in detection allows misalignment to persist, increasing the potential for instability to develop before the system adjusts.

Once a shock occurs, it does not remain confined to the point of interruption. It propagates through the structure of the income system. The path of this propagation is determined by the arrangement of layers and the distribution of dependency within the system. When the primary layer is affected, the impact is immediate and large in scale, as the system loses a significant portion of its inflow. The secondary layer then becomes more prominent, absorbing part of the load that was previously carried by the primary layer. The supplemental layer may also respond by providing flexibility, but its capacity is limited.

Propagation reflects the redistribution of pressure within the system. The loss or reduction of inflow in one component forces other components to compensate. This compensation is not equal across layers. Each layer has a defined role and a limited capacity to expand beyond that role. The secondary layer can partially offset the loss of the primary layer, but it cannot fully replace it. The supplemental layer can absorb variability, but it cannot sustain the system at scale. The system therefore experiences a shift in load, where the remaining components are required to operate under increased demand.

This redistribution introduces strain. The system attempts to maintain continuity by reallocating its existing resources, but the effectiveness of this process depends on the relationship between shock magnitude and system capacity. When the shock is small relative to the system's capacity, the redistribution can be absorbed. The system continues to function with limited disruption. When the shock is moderate, the system enters a state of strain, where the remaining components operate near their limits. When the shock is large, the system cannot compensate fully, and instability becomes more pronounced.

The temporal dimension of shock further complicates this process. The effects of a shock are not confined to the moment of interruption. They unfold over time as the system adjusts to the new conditions. Immediate effects may include the absence of expected inflow, but secondary effects emerge as the system attempts to redistribute load and maintain function. These effects may include increasing pressure on remaining components, reduced flexibility, and the gradual erosion of system stability. The full impact of a shock is therefore revealed through its progression rather than through its initial occurrence.

The interaction between layers under shock conditions highlights the differentiated roles within the system. When the primary layer is disrupted, the system experiences a reduction in scale, as the largest component of inflow is affected. When the secondary layer is disrupted, the system becomes more concentrated, increasing its dependency on the primary layer. When the supplemental layer is disrupted, the system loses flexibility, reducing its ability to respond to variation. Each layer contributes differently to stability, and the impact of its disruption reflects its role within the structure.

Shock events may also interact with each other. Multiple shocks can occur sequentially or overlap in time, creating a condition of shock stacking. In sequential shocks, the system experiences a series of interruptions, each of which reduces its capacity to respond to subsequent events. The recovery from one shock may be incomplete when the next occurs, leading to cumulative strain. In overlapping shocks, multiple interruptions affect the system simultaneously, amplifying their combined impact. In both cases, the system's ability to maintain continuity is reduced because its capacity is already engaged in responding to prior disruptions.

The distinction between shock and variability remains critical in this context. Variability represents expected deviation within a functioning system, while shock represents a structural break that alters the system's operating conditions. Confusing the two leads to misinterpretation of system behavior. Treating shock as variability delays recognition of the need for structural adjustment, while treating variability as shock may lead to unnecessary responses. The system's ability to distinguish between these conditions influences how effectively it can respond to disruption.

Following a shock, the system enters a new operating state. This state is defined by the altered conditions created by the interruption. The system is no longer operating under its previous assumptions of continuity. Instead, it must function with reduced or altered inflow, redistributed load, and increased strain on its components. This transition is not necessarily temporary. Depending on the nature of the shock, the system may not return to its prior state. The structure that existed before the interruption may no longer be viable, and the system must adapt within its constraints.

The duration of the shock introduces an additional dimension to system behavior. An interruption that is brief in duration affects the system differently than one that persists over time. In a short-duration shock, the system's response is oriented toward absorption. Existing layers and reserves are used to maintain continuity until the interruption resolves. The structure remains largely intact, and the system's behavior is defined by its ability to bridge the gap created by the temporary loss of inflow.

When the shock persists, the system can no longer rely on temporary absorption. The interruption transitions from a short-term deviation to a sustained condition. At this point, the system must operate under the assumption that the altered inflow will continue. The response shifts from absorption to adjustment, where the system attempts to realign its structure with the new conditions. This shift is constrained by the limits established in prior chapters, including capacity, coordination, and path dependence.

This distinction creates a threshold effect within the system. A shock that initially appears temporary may extend beyond the system's ability to absorb it without structural change. As duration increases, the system moves from a state of managed disruption to one of structural strain. The same interruption, differing only in duration, can therefore produce fundamentally different outcomes. Duration determines whether the system treats the shock as a transient event or as a condition requiring reconfiguration.

The interaction between duration and capacity further defines this behavior. A system with sufficient capacity may absorb longer interruptions without immediate structural change, while a system operating near its limits may require adjustment even for short-duration shocks. The outcome is therefore not determined by duration alone, but by the relationship between duration and the system's ability to sustain continuity during the interruption.

The capacity of the system to respond to shock is limited by the constraints that govern its operation. The ability to adjust layering, to modify redundancy, or to reallocate resources is restricted by factors such as capacity, coordination limits, and the persistence of prior structural decisions. The system cannot fully reconfigure itself in response to every disruption. Its response is therefore partial, shaped by the limits of its structure. These limits determine how effectively the system can absorb and respond to shock.

Income shock reveals the boundaries of the system. It exposes the extent to which the structure can absorb disruption, the capacity of its components to compensate, and the limits imposed by constraint. The system's behavior under shock conditions reflects the interaction of all previously defined elements, including dependency, capability, layering, redundancy, and constraint. These elements do not operate independently. They converge under stress, determining how the system responds to interruption.

The occurrence of shock transforms the system from a state defined by continuity to one defined by response. The focus shifts from how income is structured to how that structure behaves under disruption. The system must operate within its limits, redistributing load, absorbing strain, and attempting to maintain function. The outcome of this process depends on the relationship between the magnitude of the shock and the capacity of the system to respond. This relationship defines whether the system stabilizes in its new state or continues to deteriorate.

Shock therefore functions as the mechanism through which system limits become visible. It is not the cause of instability in isolation, but the event that reveals the system's underlying capacity and constraints. The structure that appeared stable under continuous conditions is tested, and its weaknesses are exposed. The system's response to this test determines its subsequent behavior.

Recovery and Replaceability

Income systems do not return to stability at the moment disruption ends. The period following a shock is defined not by restoration, but by transition. Recovery is the process through which a system moves from a disrupted state toward a condition that can sustain continuity. This movement is not instantaneous and does not imply a return to the prior structure. Recovery is therefore not a reversal of shock, but a time-dependent process through which the system establishes a new operating condition.

Recovery must be understood as a progression across time. It unfolds through stages in which the system absorbs the initial disruption, reallocates internal capacity, and attempts to reestablish continuity. These stages are not discrete or uniform. They overlap and interact, producing a gradual shift in system behavior rather than a clear transition from instability to stability. The system may appear stable at certain points within this process, but this appearance reflects temporary alignment rather than full restoration. Time defines the path of recovery, and the duration of this path determines the level of strain imposed on the system.

The rate at which recovery occurs introduces an additional dimension to system behavior. Two systems experiencing similar disruptions may differ significantly in how quickly they move toward stabilization. This difference is not determined solely by the magnitude of the shock, but by the system's capacity to reallocate resources, coordinate replacement, and restore alignment across components. Recovery rate reflects how efficiently the system can translate available capacity into structural adjustment over time.

A slower rate of recovery extends the period during which the system operates under reduced conditions. This extension increases cumulative strain, as components are required to sustain elevated loads for longer durations. A faster rate compresses this period, limiting the accumulation of strain and reducing the likelihood of secondary instability. The same level of disruption can therefore produce different outcomes depending on how quickly the system is able to respond.

Recovery rate is constrained by the same factors that limit adjustment more broadly. Coordination requirements, capacity ceilings, and the complexity of replacement all influence how quickly change can occur. The system cannot accelerate recovery beyond these limits. As a result, recovery is shaped not only by whether replacement is possible, but by how rapidly that replacement can be achieved within the system's constraints.

The distinction between partial and full recovery emerges from this time-based process. Full recovery would imply that the system returns to its prior structure, with the same distribution of inflows, the same dependency relationships, and the same functional capacity. In practice, this condition is uncommon. More frequently, systems achieve partial recovery, where continuity is restored but the structure is altered. The system stabilizes at a lower level of function or with a different configuration of components. The prior state is not reestablished; instead, a new equilibrium is formed under modified conditions.

This outcome reflects the influence of path dependence. Recovery does not occur from an ideal starting point, but from the system's existing state following disruption. The structure that remains after shock constrains the range of possible recovery paths. Components that were lost cannot be restored without replacement, and the process of replacement is itself subject to limitations. The system's prior decisions, including its dependency structure and capacity limits, shape the recovery process. As a result, recovery is not a process of optimization, but of adaptation within constraint.

Central to this adaptation is the concept of replaceability. Replaceability refers to the system's ability to restore lost inflow by substituting it with new inflow that fulfills the same function. It is not defined by the addition of income in general, but by the restoration of specific roles within the system. Income components differ in the functions they perform, and these functions determine how easily they can be replaced. Replaceability is therefore a structural property of income, reflecting how dependent the system is on particular inflows and how transferable those functions are.

A critical distinction exists between numerical and functional replacement. Numerical replacement occurs when the total amount of lost income is restored, regardless of its source or role. Functional replacement occurs when the specific role of the lost income is restored within the system. These two forms of replacement are not equivalent. A system may replace the numerical value of lost income without restoring its functional contribution. For example, replacing a large, stable inflow with multiple smaller, variable inflows may restore total income while altering the system's structure and behavior. Functional replacement requires alignment with the role that the original component performed, not just equivalence in magnitude.

The difficulty of replacement varies across income components. Inflows that are highly specific in their role, concentrated in their contribution, or dependent on narrow conditions are more difficult to replace. Their loss creates a gap that cannot be easily filled by alternative pathways. In contrast, inflows that are more general in function or distributed across multiple sources are more replaceable. The system's dependency structure, as well as the flexibility of its underlying capability, determines how easily replacement can occur. Replaceability is therefore not uniform across the system, but varies according to the characteristics of each component.

Time interacts with replaceability to define the recovery process. Replacement does not occur at the moment of loss. There is a delay between the disruption of inflow and the establishment of a substitute. This delay represents a period during which the system operates with reduced capacity. The length of this period, combined with the difficulty of achieving replacement, determines the level of instability experienced during recovery. A system with high replaceability may still experience strain if replacement takes time, while a system with low replaceability may experience prolonged instability even if replacement is attempted immediately.

The recovery timeline reflects this interaction between time and replaceability. Following shock, the system enters an immediate phase in which it responds to the loss of inflow through internal adjustments. This phase is characterized by attempts to maintain continuity using existing components. It is followed by a period of attempted replacement, during which the system seeks to restore lost functions. The outcome of this period determines whether the system stabilizes at a new level or continues to experience instability. Stabilization occurs when the system reaches a configuration that can sustain continuity under the new conditions.

Recovery takes place under the constraints that define the system's capacity. The system must continue to operate while simultaneously attempting to recover. This creates a condition in which resources are divided between maintaining current function and restoring lost capacity. The effort required to replace income is not separate from the effort required to sustain the system. Both processes draw on the same limited capacity, creating friction. This friction slows recovery and increases the duration of instability.

This dual demand introduces a trade-off within the recovery process. The system must balance the need to maintain continuity with the need to rebuild structure. Prioritizing immediate function may limit the resources available for replacement, prolonging the recovery process. Prioritizing replacement may reduce the system's ability to sustain itself in the short term. The system cannot fully optimize both objectives simultaneously. Recovery therefore involves a reallocation of capacity that reflects these competing demands.

In some cases, recovery does not result in restoration. The system may fail to replace lost inflow, leading to a condition of permanent degradation. In this state, the system stabilizes at a lower level of function, with reduced capacity and increased dependency on remaining components. Structural simplification may occur as the system reduces its complexity in response to the loss of capacity. Dependency may become more concentrated as fewer components carry a greater share of the system's function. This outcome reflects the limits of replaceability and the constraints on recovery.

Even when recovery appears to occur, it may not restore the system's original stability. A condition of false recovery can emerge, where the system regains continuity but with increased fragility. The new structure may rely more heavily on fewer components, reducing redundancy. It may exhibit less flexibility, making it more sensitive to future disruptions. The system appears stable because continuity has been restored, but its underlying resilience has diminished. This distinction between apparent stability and structural stability is critical in understanding post-recovery conditions.

Replacement itself may introduce new imbalances. When a lost component is replaced, the substitute may not align perfectly with the original function. Differences in timing, magnitude, or reliability can alter the system's behavior. These differences create new structural relationships, which may introduce additional sources of instability. The system adapts to these changes, but the resulting configuration is not identical to the prior state. Replacement therefore contributes to the evolution of the system rather than its restoration.

The limits of recovery are defined by the interaction of time, capacity, structure, and replaceability. Time determines how long the system must operate under reduced conditions. Capacity determines how much effort can be directed toward recovery. Structure determines the pathways available for replacement. Replaceability determines how easily lost functions can be restored. These factors interact to define the boundaries of the recovery process. Within these boundaries, the system can stabilize. Outside them, instability persists or deepens.

Resilience emerges from this interaction as a measurable property of the system. It is not defined by the absence of disruption, but by the system's ability to restore continuity within its constraints. A resilient system is one that can absorb the effects of shock, replace lost functions, and stabilize in a new operating state within a limited timeframe. This definition emphasizes process rather than outcome. Resilience is expressed through the system's behavior over time, not through its initial resistance to disruption.

The system that emerges from recovery is not identical to the system that existed before shock. It reflects the cumulative effects of disruption, replacement, and constraint. The new equilibrium incorporates the changes introduced during the recovery process, including any reductions in capacity, shifts in dependency, or alterations in structure. Stability in this context is not a return to a prior condition, but the establishment of a new condition that can be sustained.

Recovery therefore represents a transition rather than a restoration. It reveals the extent to which the system can adapt to disruption within its limits. Some systems regain continuity quickly, with minimal structural change. Others require extended periods of adjustment, during which instability persists. Some systems do not recover fully, stabilizing at reduced levels of function or remaining in a state of ongoing strain. These outcomes reflect differences in replaceability, capacity, and structural configuration.

There exists a threshold beyond which recovery transitions from difficult to unattainable. As disruption persists and capacity is depleted, the system may lose the conditions required to support replacement. Components that would have enabled recovery are themselves degraded or removed, and the system's ability to reorganize declines. At this point, the pathway back to prior levels of function is no longer available within the system's constraints.

This threshold is not defined by a single event, but by the accumulation of strain over time. As recovery is delayed and resources are consumed, the system moves closer to a state in which restoration is no longer feasible. The transition may not be immediately visible, as the system can continue to operate in a degraded condition. However, the structural conditions required for recovery have already been lost.

Beyond this point, the system no longer moves toward recovery, but toward stabilization at a lower level or continued deterioration. Replacement may still occur in limited forms, but it does not restore the original structure. The system adapts to its constrained state rather than reversing it. Irreversibility therefore represents the boundary at which recovery ceases to be a viable outcome within the system's existing configuration.

The defining characteristic of recovery is that it is neither guaranteed nor uniform. It depends on the interaction of multiple factors that determine whether lost income can be replaced and how long that replacement takes. The system's ability to navigate this process determines its resilience. Recovery is therefore not an assumption, but a condition that must be achieved within the constraints of the system.

Continuity and Durability

Continuity defines whether an income system remains operational across time. It is not the absence of disruption, nor the elimination of variability, but the ability of the system to maintain function despite these conditions. Income systems are inherently exposed to timing irregularities, interruptions, and structural changes. Continuity reflects whether these disruptions result in a breakdown of function or whether the system continues to operate through them. The presence of continuity indicates that inflow, even if altered, remains sufficient in structure and sequence to sustain the system's operation.

This distinction separates continuity from stability as it is often perceived. A system may appear stable at a given moment while lacking continuity across time. Stability observed at a single point does not account for the system's ability to withstand interruption or variation. Continuity, by contrast, is observable only through persistence. It requires that the system function across multiple periods, including those in which conditions deviate from expectation. The system's capacity to maintain operation through these deviations defines its continuity.

Durability extends this concept by introducing resistance to structural breakdown. While continuity describes ongoing function, durability describes the system's ability to sustain that function under stress. A system may maintain continuity under normal conditions yet fail when exposed to disruption. Durability distinguishes between systems that can operate continuously in stable environments and those that can maintain continuity when conditions change. It is therefore not a short-term property, but a structural one, defined by how the system behaves when subjected to pressure.

The distinction between durability and short-term stability becomes evident when systems encounter disruption. A system that appears stable may do so because it has not yet been tested. Its structure may depend on conditions that remain unchanged, masking underlying fragility. When those conditions shift, the system's lack of durability becomes visible. Durability is therefore not inferred from stability observed in isolation, but from the system's response to variation, interruption, and shock. Time reveals this distinction by exposing the system to changing conditions.

The mechanisms that challenge continuity have been established in earlier structural analysis. Variability introduces deviations in timing and magnitude, testing whether the system can maintain alignment across periods. Sequence mismatch creates gaps where inflows do not coincide with obligations, disrupting function even when total income is sufficient. Interruption introduces absence within the sequence, forcing the system to operate without replenishment. Shock represents the structural break in continuity, while recovery determines whether function can be restored. Each of these mechanisms tests the system's ability to sustain operation across time. Durability is defined by the system's performance under these conditions.

The transition from recovery to durability marks a shift in focus from restoration to persistence. Recovery describes the process through which the system reestablishes continuity following disruption. It addresses whether lost function can be replaced and how long that replacement takes. Durability, by contrast, addresses whether the system can maintain continuity after recovery. A system may recover from disruption and yet remain fragile, susceptible to further breakdown under subsequent stress. Durability determines whether recovery leads to sustained function or whether the system remains vulnerable.

Structural survival emerges from the interaction of the system's components. The arrangement of income into layers distributes function across different inflows, allowing the system to absorb disruption without complete failure. Redundancy provides alternative pathways through which income can be maintained, reducing dependency on any single component. Replaceability determines whether lost inflows can be substituted, allowing recovery to occur. These elements do not guarantee durability, but they define the system's capacity for survival. A system lacking these structural features may function under stable conditions but will struggle to persist when those conditions change.

Durability is therefore not a property of individual components, but of their arrangement. A system composed of multiple inflows may still lack durability if those inflows are concentrated in their dependency or limited in their replaceability. Conversely, a system with fewer components may exhibit durability if those components are adaptable and distributed in their function. The structural configuration determines how the system responds to disruption, and therefore whether continuity can be maintained across time.

Adaptation plays a central role in this process. Systems must change in order to persist, but this change must occur without breaking continuity. Adaptation involves the reconfiguration of components in response to new conditions, allowing the system to maintain function even as its structure evolves. This process is constrained by the limits established in earlier analysis. Capacity, coordination, and prior structural decisions restrict the extent to which the system can adapt. Durability depends on whether adaptation can occur within these constraints without producing further instability.

Fragility represents the absence of this capacity. A fragile system is one that breaks under change, where disruption leads to a loss of function that cannot be sustained or restored. Fragility is not defined solely by the occurrence of failure, but by the system's inability to maintain continuity when conditions shift. Durable systems, by contrast, absorb change and continue to operate, even if their structure is altered. The distinction between fragility and durability is therefore observed in the system's response to change rather than in its behavior under stable conditions.

Time serves as the final filter through which durability is measured. Stability observed over a short period does not indicate durability. Only systems that maintain continuity across extended periods, including those characterized by disruption and change, demonstrate durability. Time exposes the cumulative effects of variability, dependency, constraint, and shock. Systems that appear stable in the short term may degrade over longer horizons, revealing structural weaknesses that were not immediately apparent. Durability is therefore established through persistence, not through initial performance.

This temporal dimension introduces a threshold for persistence. Systems may achieve temporary stability following recovery, but only those that sustain function across subsequent periods can be considered durable. This threshold is not defined by a specific duration, but by the system's ability to maintain continuity as conditions evolve. The system must operate through multiple cycles of variation and disruption without losing function. Durability is confirmed when continuity persists despite these repeated challenges.

Durability is not established through a single period of successful operation, nor through a single recovery following disruption. It is tested through repeated exposure to variation, interruption, and structural change. Each cycle of disruption imposes strain on the system, requiring it to absorb, adjust, and continue functioning. A system that maintains continuity once may still fail under repeated stress if the cumulative effects of these cycles exceed its capacity to adapt. Durability therefore reflects not only the system's ability to withstand isolated events, but its ability to persist across multiple cycles of disruption without losing function. The system must sustain continuity repeatedly, not just initially, in order to demonstrate true persistence.

The interaction between continuity and durability defines the transition to true stability. Continuity ensures that the system can function across time, while durability ensures that this function can be sustained under changing conditions. Stability emerges from the combination of these properties. It is not a static condition, but a dynamic one, maintained through the system's ability to persist across variability, interruption, and adaptation. Stability therefore reflects the system's capacity to operate continuously within a changing environment.

The structural elements that support this outcome must be understood in relation to time. Layering distributes function across inflows, allowing the system to absorb disruption in the short term. Redundancy provides alternative pathways that support continuity during variation. Replaceability enables recovery following loss. Durability integrates these elements across time, determining whether the system can maintain function as conditions change. Each element contributes to stability, but only durability ensures that this stability persists.

The system's behavior under change ultimately determines its quality. Systems that maintain continuity only under stable conditions exhibit a form of conditional stability that does not extend across time. Systems that persist through disruption demonstrate durability, reflecting a deeper level of structural integrity. The distinction between these states becomes evident only through observation across multiple periods. Time reveals whether the system can sustain function or whether it will degrade.

Persistence over time does not imply that the system remains unchanged. Even in the absence of visible disruption, structural erosion may occur as components weaken, dependencies concentrate, or flexibility diminishes. This erosion is often gradual and may not produce immediate failure, allowing the system to continue operating while its underlying resilience declines. Each period of operation under strain can reduce the system's capacity to absorb future disruption, creating a condition in which durability decreases over time. The system may appear stable because continuity is maintained, yet its ability to persist under subsequent stress is reduced. Durability must therefore be understood not only as the ability to sustain function, but as the ability to do so without progressive loss of structural integrity.

Continuity maintained under strain does not guarantee long-term durability. A system may continue to operate despite progressive erosion, creating the appearance of persistence while its underlying capacity declines. This condition produces delayed failure, where the system remains functional for a period of time before reaching a threshold beyond which continuity can no longer be sustained. The absence of immediate breakdown can obscure the accumulation of structural weakness, allowing the system to operate in a degraded state without visible collapse.

This delayed failure reflects a divergence between observable continuity and underlying durability. The system appears stable because inflow continues and obligations are met, yet the conditions required to sustain that function are deteriorating. As capacity diminishes and flexibility is reduced, the system becomes increasingly sensitive to disruption. A shock that could previously have been absorbed may now exceed the system's reduced capacity, resulting in failure that appears sudden but is in fact the result of accumulated strain.

Durability therefore cannot be evaluated solely on the presence of continuity at a given point in time. It must account for the trajectory of the system's structure and its capacity to sustain function under future conditions. A system that maintains continuity while its structural integrity declines is not durable, but temporarily stable. The distinction between these states becomes visible only when the system is exposed to additional stress, revealing whether continuity can still be maintained or whether the accumulated erosion results in breakdown.

Continuity and durability therefore represent the final stage in the evaluation of income systems. They synthesize the mechanisms that define system behavior and apply them across time. Continuity measures whether the system remains operational, while durability measures whether this operation can be sustained. Together, they define the conditions under which stability exists. Stability is not achieved when the system appears balanced, but when it remains functional despite the presence of change.

The resulting framework positions durability as the determining factor in long-term stability. Systems that lack durability may function temporarily, but they do not persist. Systems that exhibit durability maintain continuity across changing conditions, demonstrating the capacity to survive disruption and adapt within constraint. Stability is therefore not a momentary state, but a condition proven over time.

Income → Liquidity → Runway

Income operates as a flow, not as a fixed quantity. It enters the system across time, arriving in sequences that may vary in magnitude, timing, and reliability. This flow sustains the system only to the extent that it can be converted into usable capacity. The presence of income alone does not determine stability. What matters is how that flow is transformed into a form that can support ongoing operation when conditions change. The system depends not on the existence of inflow at a given moment, but on its ability to translate that inflow into continuity across time.

Liquidity serves as the conversion layer between income and system function. It represents the portion of inflow that has been retained in a form that can be deployed when needed. This retained capacity allows the system to operate independently of the exact timing of income. Without liquidity, the system is bound to the sequence of inflows, requiring precise alignment between income and obligations. With liquidity, the system gains the ability to absorb timing differences, smoothing the irregularities inherent in income flow. Liquidity does not create income, but it determines how effectively income can be used.

This conversion is necessary because income does not arrive continuously. Even in systems with predictable inflow, there are intervals between receipts. During these intervals, the system must continue to function. Liquidity bridges these intervals, providing continuity in the absence of immediate inflow. It transforms discrete income events into a sustained capacity to operate. The system's stability therefore depends not only on how much income is generated, but on how much of that income is retained as liquidity and how effectively that liquidity can be deployed.

Runway emerges from this conversion as a measure of time. It represents the duration for which the system can continue to operate in the absence of inflow. Runway is not an abstract concept, but a direct expression of liquidity in temporal terms. It answers the question of how long the system can sustain its obligations without additional income. This duration defines the system's survival capacity under constraint. A system with extended runway can continue to function through periods of interruption or variability. A system with limited runway faces immediate pressure when inflow is disrupted.

The relationship between income, liquidity, and runway forms a continuous chain. Income generates the flow that feeds the system. Liquidity captures a portion of that flow and stores it as usable capacity. Runway converts that capacity into time, representing how long the system can sustain itself without additional inflow. Each stage in this chain depends on the previous one, and any disruption in the chain affects the system's ability to maintain continuity.

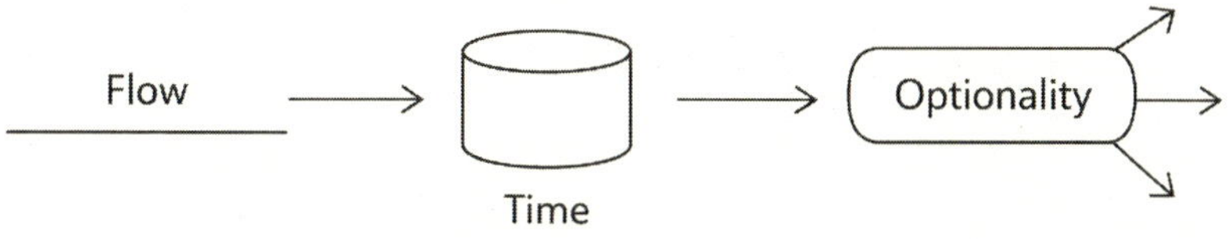

Figure 11 – Flow → Time → Optionality

This chain establishes the foundation for understanding how instability affects the system. Variability in income reduces the efficiency of conversion. When inflow is irregular, the system must rely more heavily on liquidity to maintain continuity. This increases the rate at which liquidity is consumed, shortening runway. Timing mismatches further exacerbate this effect. When income does not align with obligations, liquidity must compensate, even if total income remains unchanged. These mismatches create friction within the system, accelerating the depletion of stored capacity.

Gaps in income introduce a more direct form of strain. During periods with no inflow, the system operates entirely on liquidity. The duration of these gaps determines how quickly runway is reduced. Short gaps may be absorbed with minimal impact, but extended gaps result in sustained drawdown. The system's survival becomes a function of how long liquidity can support operation in the absence of income. As runway shortens, the system approaches a condition where continuity cannot be maintained.

Shock events produce the most immediate effect on runway. A sudden interruption in income eliminates expected inflow, forcing the system to rely entirely on liquidity. The rate of depletion increases sharply, as the system must sustain itself without replenishment. The magnitude of the shock determines how quickly runway is consumed. Large shocks can reduce runway rapidly, while smaller shocks produce more gradual effects. In both cases, the system transitions from a state of flow-supported operation to one dependent on stored capacity.

The dynamics of runway depletion are not linear. Small changes in income stability can produce disproportionately large effects on runway. Variability that increases the frequency or magnitude of drawdowns reduces the efficiency of liquidity usage. Gaps that extend slightly beyond expected durations can accelerate depletion in ways that are not immediately apparent. Shock events can trigger rapid declines that exceed initial expectations. The system's time capacity is therefore sensitive to changes in flow, and this sensitivity introduces nonlinearity into the relationship between income and runway.

This nonlinearity becomes critical when the system approaches the limits of its runway. As liquidity decreases, each additional unit of time becomes more difficult to sustain. The system's margin for absorbing further instability diminishes, and the rate of depletion may increase. This creates a condition in which runway appears sufficient until it reaches a threshold, beyond which it collapses rapidly. The system does not lose time gradually in all cases; it may experience a compression of its remaining capacity as instability compounds.

The reduction of runway introduces pressure into the system. Pressure is not defined by the presence of instability alone, but by the interaction between instability and limited time. As runway shortens, the system has less capacity to absorb variation or delay. The consequences of each disruption become more immediate, and the system must respond within a narrower time frame. This compression of time alters the system's behavior, as decisions must be made under increasing constraint.

This leads to the formation of a feedback loop that reinforces instability. As instability reduces runway, the system experiences increased pressure. This pressure affects the quality of decisions made within the system. Decisions made under constrained time are more likely to prioritize immediate continuity over long-term stability. These decisions may increase dependency, reduce flexibility, or introduce additional variability. As a result, the system becomes more unstable, further reducing runway and increasing pressure. The loop continues, with each cycle reinforcing the conditions that produced it.

The feedback loop can be expressed as a sequence of interactions. Instability reduces runway by increasing the rate of liquidity depletion. Reduced runway compresses the time available for decision-making, increasing pressure. Increased pressure leads to decisions that may degrade system structure, such as concentrating dependency or reducing adaptability. These structural changes introduce additional instability, which further accelerates the depletion of runway. The system becomes caught in a cycle where instability and time compression reinforce each other.

This loop illustrates that instability is not confined to income flow alone. It extends into the system's ability to manage itself. As runway decreases, the system's capacity to respond effectively diminishes. The interaction between structural limitations and time constraints becomes the defining factor in system behavior. Stability is therefore not only a function of income structure, but of the system's position within this feedback loop.

Optionality emerges as the outcome of this dynamic. Optionality represents the range of choices available to the system in response to changing conditions. It is directly tied to runway, as the availability of time determines whether the system can consider multiple pathways or is forced into immediate action. A system with extended runway has the capacity to evaluate alternatives, adjust its structure, and respond to instability with flexibility. A system with limited runway must act within narrow constraints, often selecting options that preserve short-term continuity at the expense of long-term stability.

The collapse of optionality occurs when runway becomes insufficient to support deliberation. Decisions are no longer guided by structural considerations, but by the need to maintain immediate function. This shift alters the system's trajectory, as it prioritizes survival over optimization. The range of possible actions narrows, and the system becomes more rigid in its responses. This rigidity can further increase instability, as the system loses the ability to adapt effectively to changing conditions.

The relationship between runway and optionality reinforces the importance of time within the system. Time is not simply a measure of duration, but a resource that determines the system's capacity for adaptation. Extended runway expands this resource, allowing the system to operate with greater flexibility. Reduced runway constrains it, limiting the system's ability to respond to instability. The conversion of income into time therefore becomes a central determinant of system behavior.

Stability can be understood as the expansion of time capacity within this framework. Stable income structures produce consistent flow, allowing liquidity to accumulate and runway to extend. This extended runway reduces pressure, enabling the system to operate with greater optionality. The feedback loop that amplifies instability is weakened, as the system has sufficient time to absorb variation and adjust its structure. Stability is therefore not defined by the absence of disruption, but by the presence of sufficient time to manage it.

This perspective reframes income stability as a function of time rather than magnitude. The amount of income generated is relevant only to the extent that it contributes to liquidity and runway. Systems with identical income levels may exhibit different stability profiles depending on how effectively they convert income into time. A system with efficient conversion and extended runway can maintain continuity under a wide range of conditions. A system with inefficient conversion and limited runway may experience instability even with higher income.

The full model integrates these relationships into a coherent structure. Income generates flow, which is captured as liquidity. Liquidity defines runway, representing the system's time capacity. Runway determines optionality, shaping the system's ability to respond to instability. Instability reduces runway, compressing time and increasing pressure. Pressure influences decisions, which in turn affect income structure and stability. The system operates within this cycle, with time as the central variable that connects its components.

The transformation of income into time establishes the link between financial structure and system behavior. Income is not an end state, but the input that determines how much time the system has to operate under constraint. Liquidity translates this input into usable capacity, and runway expresses it as duration. The system's stability depends on how this duration interacts with the conditions it faces. When time is sufficient, the system can absorb and adapt. When time is limited, the system is forced into reactive behavior that may increase instability.

This framework positions runway as the bridge between income and decision freedom. The length of runway determines whether the system operates with flexibility or under constraint. It defines the boundary between deliberate adaptation and forced response. As such, runway is not merely a measure of survival, but a determinant of system quality. Systems with extended runway exhibit greater resilience and adaptability, while those with limited runway are more susceptible to instability.

The final implication is that instability is experienced as a loss of time. Variability, gaps, and shock all reduce the system's runway, compressing the period over which it can operate without disruption. This compression increases pressure and reduces optionality, reinforcing the conditions that produce instability. Stability, in contrast, is experienced as the preservation and extension of time. The system gains the capacity to operate across a broader range of conditions, maintaining continuity without immediate constraint.

Income, liquidity, and runway therefore form a unified system in which financial flow is converted into temporal capacity. This capacity defines the system's ability to sustain itself, adapt to change, and maintain stability. The interaction between flow, buffer, and time determines whether the system operates under pressure or with flexibility. The outcome of this interaction shapes the system's behavior across all conditions, establishing time as the central dimension of income stability.

Income and Expense Alignment

Income and expenses operate as two distinct systems within a household financial structure. Each has its own behavior, timing, and internal logic. Income enters the system as a flow, varying across time in magnitude and arrival. It may be stable or irregular, concentrated or distributed, predictable or uncertain. Expenses, by contrast, function as structured outflows. They are defined by recurrence, obligation, and timing rigidity. While income adapts to conditions, expenses often persist independently of them. The interaction between these two systems determines whether continuity can be maintained.

The distinction between these systems is structural rather than incidental. Income behaves dynamically, reflecting variability in timing and amount. Expenses behave rigidly, anchored to schedules and obligations that do not adjust automatically in response to income conditions. This asymmetry creates the foundation for potential instability. The system must reconcile a flexible inflow with a fixed outflow, and the degree to which these structures align determines whether that reconciliation is sustainable.

Alignment refers to the compatibility between the structure of income and the structure of expenses. It is not a matter of whether income exceeds expenses in aggregate, but whether the characteristics of inflow match the requirements of outflow. This compatibility operates across multiple dimensions. Timing must align so that inflows arrive when obligations are due. Variability must align so that fluctuations in income do not exceed the system's capacity to absorb them. Magnitude must align so that inflow is sufficient to sustain required outflow. When these conditions are met, the system can operate with reduced friction. When they are not, instability emerges.

The mismatch between fixed expenses and variable income illustrates the core mechanism of misalignment. Fixed obligations persist regardless of changes in income. They do not adjust downward when inflow decreases, nor do they shift in timing to accommodate delays. Income, however, may fluctuate in both magnitude and timing. When a variable inflow must support fixed outflows, the system experiences asymmetric stress. The burden of adjustment falls entirely on the income side, while expenses remain unchanged. This asymmetry amplifies the impact of variability, as any reduction or delay in income directly affects the system's ability to meet obligations.

This condition does not require extreme variation to produce instability. Even moderate fluctuations in income can create stress when paired with rigid expenses. The system must continuously compensate for these fluctuations, drawing on available resources to maintain alignment. The effect is cumulative. Each instance of mismatch requires adjustment, and repeated adjustments introduce persistent pressure into the system. The instability is not episodic but continuous, arising from the ongoing incompatibility between inflow and outflow structures.

Timing misalignment introduces an additional layer of complexity. Income may be sufficient in total but arrive at intervals that do not coincide with the timing of obligations. Expenses are often due at fixed points, creating discrete moments where outflow is required. If income arrives before or after these moments, the system must bridge the gap. This gap represents a form of sequence mismatch, where the order of inflows and outflows determines whether obligations can be met. The system's success depends not on the total amount of income, but on its alignment with the sequence of expenses.

This temporal mismatch reinforces the structural incompatibility between income and expenses. Even in systems where income is relatively stable, differences in timing can produce periods of insufficiency. The system must then rely on stored capacity to maintain continuity. The need for this compensation arises not from a lack of income, but from the misalignment of its arrival with the system's obligations. Timing, therefore, becomes as critical as magnitude in determining stability.

Liquidity functions as the mechanism through which the system compensates for these mismatches. It provides a buffer that allows the system to operate independently of exact alignment between inflow and outflow. When income arrives early, liquidity stores the excess for future use. When income arrives late or is reduced, liquidity provides the necessary capacity to meet obligations. This buffering effect enables the system to maintain continuity despite structural differences between income and expenses.

However, liquidity does not resolve the underlying mismatch. It absorbs the effects of misalignment, but it does not eliminate them. Each instance of compensation reduces the available buffer, drawing down the system's stored capacity. When mismatches occur repeatedly, this drawdown becomes persistent. The system relies increasingly on liquidity to maintain alignment, and the available runway decreases. The presence of liquidity masks the structural issue temporarily, but the underlying incompatibility remains.

This leads to a condition of continuous stress. Misalignment is not a discrete event but an ongoing process. Each period in which income and expenses fail to align requires compensation. The system must continually adjust, drawing on liquidity to bridge gaps in timing, magnitude, or variability. This repeated adjustment creates a steady state of pressure, where the system operates near the limits of its capacity. The stress is not caused by a single disruption, but by the persistence of structural mismatch.

The interaction between misalignment and liquidity produces a reinforcing loop. When income and expenses are misaligned, liquidity is used to compensate. This reduces runway, shortening the time the system can sustain itself without additional inflow. As runway decreases, the system becomes more sensitive to further mismatches. Each subsequent instance of misalignment has a greater impact, as the buffer available to absorb it is smaller. The system enters a cycle where misalignment leads to depletion, and depletion increases the effects of misalignment.

This loop illustrates that misalignment is not self-correcting. Without structural adjustment, the system does not naturally return to equilibrium. Instead, the effects accumulate, increasing pressure over time. The system may appear stable while liquidity remains sufficient, but this stability is conditional. It depends on the continued availability of a buffer that is being gradually depleted. When that buffer reaches its limit, the underlying mismatch becomes fully exposed, and continuity is disrupted.

The degree of alignment can be understood as a gradient rather than a binary condition. Systems that exhibit full alignment, where income and expenses match in timing, variability, and magnitude, experience minimal structural friction. These systems operate with low stress, as inflows naturally meet outflows without requiring significant compensation. Systems with partial alignment experience manageable stress, where occasional mismatches are absorbed without persistent strain. Systems with significant misalignment operate under continuous pressure, where compensation is required in each period and instability is ongoing.

This gradient highlights that alignment is not an absolute state but a relative one. Improvements in alignment reduce the frequency and magnitude of mismatches, decreasing the system's reliance on liquidity. Deterioration in alignment increases these mismatches, amplifying the need for compensation. The system's position along this gradient determines its level of stability. Movement toward alignment reduces structural friction, while movement away from alignment increases it.

Structural alignment is most visible not in the absence of stress, but in how the system behaves under normal variation. In an aligned system, variability in income does not immediately translate into instability because the structure of expenses accommodates that variability. Fixed obligations are proportionate to the most stable components of income, while more variable inflows support flexible or discretionary outflows. This creates a distribution in which the most rigid expenses are supported by the most predictable income, reducing the likelihood that fluctuations will disrupt continuity.

Timing alignment further reinforces this structure. Inflows arrive in a sequence that corresponds to the timing of obligations, minimizing the need for compensation through liquidity. The system does not rely on buffering to maintain continuity because inflow and outflow are synchronized. When minor mismatches occur, they are absorbed without persistent drawdown, as the system's structure inherently reduces the frequency and magnitude of gaps.

Variability is also distributed across the system in a way that limits its impact. Fluctuations in income affect components of the system that can adjust in response, rather than those that are fixed. This reduces the transmission of variability into structural stress. The system does not eliminate variability, but it contains it within segments that can absorb change without disrupting overall function.

Alignment, therefore, is not a static condition but an arrangement of relationships within the system. It reflects how different types of income support different types of expenses, how timing is coordinated across inflows and outflows, and how variability is directed toward areas that can accommodate it. When these relationships are established, the system operates with reduced friction, maintaining continuity without continuous reliance on compensation.

Stability, in this context, emerges from compatibility rather than magnitude. A system with high income may still experience instability if its structure is incompatible with its expenses. Conversely, a system with lower income may maintain continuity if its inflow aligns with its obligations. The relationship between income and expenses is therefore not defined by their absolute levels, but by how their structures interact. Compatibility reduces the need for compensation, while incompatibility increases it.

The structural nature of this interaction explains why income alone is insufficient to determine stability. Income must be evaluated in relation to the system it supports. The characteristics of that system, including the rigidity of expenses and the timing of obligations, define the conditions under which income operates. Stability requires that these conditions be met not occasionally, but consistently across time. Alignment ensures that this consistency can be maintained without excessive reliance on buffering mechanisms.

The persistence of misalignment reveals the limits of compensation. Liquidity can extend the system's capacity to operate under mismatch, but it cannot sustain indefinite compensation. As the system continues to draw on its buffer, the margin for absorbing further misalignment decreases. The system becomes more vulnerable to disruption, as each new mismatch has a greater impact. The structural issue becomes increasingly dominant, eventually determining the system's behavior.

Alignment, therefore, represents the condition under which the system can operate without continuous strain. It reduces the frequency and severity of mismatches, allowing income to support expenses directly rather than through constant mediation. This reduction in structural friction preserves liquidity, extends runway, and stabilizes the system over time. Alignment does not eliminate variability or disruption, but it ensures that the system can accommodate them without persistent pressure.

The relationship between income and expenses is thus central to understanding system stability. Income provides the flow that sustains the system, while expenses define the conditions under which that flow must operate. The compatibility of these two structures determines whether continuity can be maintained. When they align, the system operates with efficiency and resilience. When they do not, the system enters a state of ongoing stress, where stability depends on temporary compensation rather than structural coherence.

The resulting framework positions alignment as a structural requirement rather than a secondary consideration. Stability is not achieved by increasing income alone, but by ensuring that the behavior of income matches the requirements of the system it supports. This matching reduces the need for compensation, preserves system capacity, and allows continuity to be maintained across time.

Income and Decision Space

Income stability ultimately expresses itself not in the amount of resources accumulated, but in the range of decisions a system can sustain over time. The concept of decision space captures this outcome. Decision space is not the set of all imaginable actions, but the set of actions that are structurally viable given current conditions. It is bounded by time, constrained by available capacity, and shaped by the interaction between inflow and obligation. What a system can do is determined less by what exists in aggregate and more by what can be executed within its constraints.

Decision space emerges as the operational consequence of income structure. It reflects the translation of financial behavior into real-world flexibility. A system with broad decision space can delay, adjust, or redirect its actions without immediate breakdown. A system with narrow decision space operates within tight constraints, where only a limited set of actions can be taken without triggering instability. The distinction between these states is not behavioral but structural. It arises from how income is generated, stored, and sustained across time.

The connection between decision space and time is direct. Time defines the window within which decisions can be made. This window is determined by runway, the duration a system can continue functioning without additional inflow. Runway converts financial capacity into temporal capacity. When runway is extended, decisions can be deferred, evaluated, and sequenced with greater precision. When runway is compressed, decisions must be made immediately, often under conditions of incomplete information and limited alternatives. The length of runway therefore sets the boundary of decision space.

This relationship positions time as the central mediator between income and decision-making. Income generates liquidity, liquidity extends runway, and runway determines the range of viable choices. The system does not act directly on income; it acts within the time created by that income. As this time expands or contracts, so does the system's ability to navigate uncertainty. Decision space is therefore not static. It expands with stability and contracts with instability, reflecting the dynamic nature of the underlying system.

Stable income structures expand decision space by preserving time. Consistency in inflow allows liquidity to accumulate or remain intact, which in turn maintains or extends runway. With sufficient runway, the system can tolerate variability, absorb temporary disruptions, and evaluate multiple courses of action. Decisions can be aligned with longer-term considerations rather than immediate necessity. The presence of time allows for sequencing, where actions can be ordered in a way that maintains continuity while adapting to changing conditions.

This expansion of decision space is not simply an increase in options, but an increase in viable options. Many theoretical choices exist in any system, but only a subset can be executed without causing instability. Stability enlarges this subset by reducing the constraints that eliminate alternatives. It allows the system to consider paths that would otherwise be inaccessible under pressure. The effect is a broader range of actions that can be taken without compromising the system's integrity.

As decision space contracts, the reduction in available options does not occur uniformly. Certain categories of decisions are eliminated earlier than others, based on their structural requirements. Actions that depend on extended time horizons, sequencing, or delayed outcomes are the first to become infeasible. These actions require sufficient runway to execute, and when that runway is reduced, they fall outside the set of viable choices.

What remains are decisions that produce immediate effects. These actions are not necessarily optimal, but they are executable within the system's constraints. The filtering process is therefore not based on preference, but on feasibility. The system does not select among all possible actions, but only among those that can be sustained within its available time and capacity.

This filtering mechanism reshapes the decision landscape. As higher-order options are removed, the system becomes increasingly reliant on actions that preserve short-term continuity. The structure of decision space changes, not only in size but in composition. What remains is a narrower set of actions oriented toward immediacy, rather than flexibility or long-term stability.

Instability produces the opposite effect. As income becomes variable, interrupted, or structurally constrained, liquidity is drawn down and runway shortens. The time available to make decisions contracts, and with it the set of viable options. Choices that require time become infeasible. Actions must be taken to maintain immediate continuity, often at the expense of longer-term stability. The system becomes reactive, responding to constraints rather than navigating within them.

This compression of decision space is not gradual in all cases. Under certain conditions, small reductions in runway can eliminate entire categories of options. Decisions that depend on flexibility, sequencing, or delayed outcomes become unavailable. The system is forced into a narrower path, where only actions that produce immediate results can be sustained. The loss of optionality is therefore nonlinear, reflecting the sensitivity of decision space to time constraints.

Constraint does not impose itself in a single step, but through a progression of increasing restriction. In the initial stage, the system retains a broad range of viable options, with sufficient runway to evaluate and sequence decisions. As runway begins to decline, flexibility is reduced, and certain actions require prioritization over others. The system must allocate its limited capacity more selectively, narrowing the range of viable choices.

As constraint intensifies, prioritization gives way to forced selection. The system can no longer consider multiple paths simultaneously and must commit to specific actions in order to maintain continuity. The margin for error decreases, and the cost of misalignment increases. Decisions become more immediate, less reversible, and more consequential.

In the final stage, constraint reaches a point where decision space collapses. The system no longer operates within a range of choices, but along a single viable path. Actions are dictated by necessity, and the system loses the ability to adjust or defer. This progression illustrates that constraint is not simply the absence of flexibility, but the gradual elimination of alternatives as time and capacity are reduced.

Pressure plays a central role in this compression. As runway decreases, the urgency of maintaining continuity increases. This urgency alters the nature of decision-making. Decisions are no longer evaluated based on their structural alignment with long-term stability, but on their ability to address immediate constraints. The system prioritizes actions that preserve short-term function, even if those actions introduce future instability. The presence of pressure reshapes the decision landscape, reducing both the number and quality of viable choices.

This distortion is structural rather than psychological. It arises from the conditions under which decisions must be made, not from individual preference or behavior. When time is limited, the system cannot accommodate actions that require extended execution or delayed outcomes. The structure of available options is altered by constraint. Decision quality declines not because of error, but because the set of viable actions has been reduced to those that address immediate needs.

The relationship between structure and decision-making reveals a form of determinism within the system. Decisions are not made in isolation but are bounded by the conditions created by income structure. The system defines what is possible before any choice is made. Income variability, timing mismatch, dependency concentration, and constraint all shape the environment in which decisions occur. The resulting decision space reflects these conditions, limiting or expanding the system's ability to act.

This structural limitation explains why similar decision processes can produce different outcomes across systems. A system with extended runway and stable inflow can select from a wide range of viable actions, while a system under constraint must operate within a narrow set of options. The difference in outcomes is not attributable to the decision process itself, but to the structure that defines what decisions are possible. Decision space therefore serves as the link between system design and system behavior.

The feedback between decisions and system stability further reinforces this relationship. Decisions made under constraint often prioritize immediate continuity, which can introduce additional instability. For example, actions that increase dependency, reduce flexibility, or compress future runway may resolve short-term pressure while degrading the system's structure. These decisions narrow future decision space, creating a cycle in which reduced optionality leads to further constraint.

This reinforcing loop can operate in both directions. In systems with sufficient runway, decisions can be made that preserve or enhance structural stability. Actions can be aligned with maintaining liquidity, extending runway, or reducing exposure to disruption. These decisions expand future decision space, creating a positive cycle where stability supports better decisions, and better decisions reinforce stability. The system's trajectory is therefore shaped by the interaction between its structure and the decisions it enables.

The distinction between these feedback loops highlights the importance of initial conditions. Systems with limited decision space are more likely to enter a cycle of degradation, where each decision reduces future optionality. Systems with expanded decision space can maintain or improve their structure over time, preserving flexibility and resilience. The divergence between these trajectories is driven by the availability of viable choices, not by the presence of different decision rules.

As decision space contracts, the nature of decisions themselves changes. In systems with sufficient optionality, decisions can be revised, reversed, or adjusted over time. The presence of runway allows for correction, enabling the system to respond to new information or changing conditions.

Under constraint, this reversibility diminishes. Decisions must be executed within limited time, and the ability to revisit those decisions is reduced. Actions taken to preserve immediate continuity often commit the system to specific structural paths. These commitments may alter dependency relationships, reduce flexibility, or introduce new constraints that cannot be easily undone.

This creates a condition in which decisions have compounding effects. Each action not only addresses current constraints but also shapes future decision space. As reversibility declines, the system becomes increasingly path dependent. The range of future options is determined by the decisions made under constraint, reinforcing the narrowing of decision space.

The result is a shift from adaptive behavior to locked trajectories. The system no longer navigates among alternatives, but moves along paths defined by prior constraints. Stability, in this context, is characterized by the preservation of reversible decisions, while instability is marked by the accumulation of irreversible commitments.

The full chain linking income to decision space clarifies this dynamic. Income enters the system as a flow, which is converted into liquidity. Liquidity extends runway, providing time under constraint. Runway determines the range of viable actions, forming the system's decision space. Each link in this chain influences the next, creating a continuous relationship between financial structure and operational behavior.

Disruptions at any point in the chain propagate through the system, altering its capacity to make decisions.

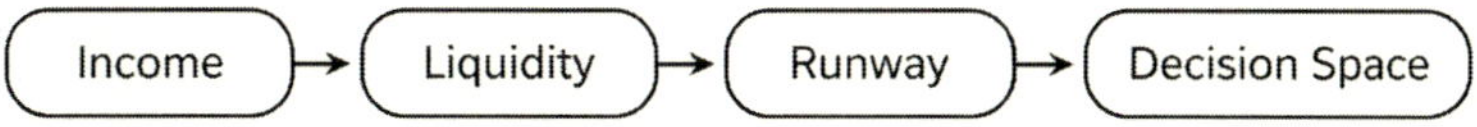

Figure 12 – Income to Decision Space Chain

This chain is not static. Variability in income affects liquidity, which alters runway. Changes in runway modify decision space, which in turn influences the decisions made. These decisions feed back into the structure of the system, affecting future income, liquidity, and runway. The system evolves through this interaction, with decision space acting as both an output and an input to its behavior.

Stability, within this framework, is defined by the preservation of decision space over time. A stable system maintains a sufficient range of viable options despite variability, disruption, and constraint. It retains the ability to adjust, sequence, and defer actions without immediate breakdown. This preservation is not absolute but relative, reflecting the system's capacity to sustain function across changing conditions.

Instability, by contrast, is characterized by the progressive reduction of decision space. As constraints accumulate, the range of viable actions narrows. The system becomes increasingly reactive, with decisions driven by necessity rather than choice. The loss of optionality signals a shift in system behavior, where continuity is maintained only through immediate and often suboptimal actions. This condition reflects the underlying structure of the system rather than its momentary state.

The translation of income into decision space therefore represents the final expression of income stability. Income determines the flow of resources, but its significance lies in how that flow is converted into time and flexibility. Time defines the system's ability to navigate uncertainty, and flexibility determines the range of actions it can sustain. Together, these factors shape the decisions that drive the system's trajectory.

The relationship between income, time, and decision space reveals that financial stability is not an abstract condition but a concrete operational reality. It is reflected in what the system can do, when it can do it, and how many alternatives it can sustain. The quality of decisions available at any moment is determined by the structure that precedes them. Income stability, therefore, is not measured solely by the presence of resources, but by the preservation of the capacity to choose among viable paths.

In this way, the system becomes self-referential. Income structure shapes decision space, decision space shapes decisions, and decisions reshape income structure. The continuity of this cycle determines whether the system maintains or loses stability over time. The preservation of decision space allows the system to navigate this cycle without degradation, while its compression leads to increasingly constrained and reactive behavior.

The final implication is that stability is experienced not as a static condition, but as an ongoing ability to choose among viable options. It is the persistence of flexibility under constraint, the retention of time under pressure, and the maintenance of alternatives under uncertainty. Income stability manifests through this preserved capacity, translating structural properties into real-world consequences that define the system's path forward.

The Continuity of Flow

Income exists as movement. It is not a fixed quantity held at a moment in time, but a sequence of inflows extending across time. This movement defines the system. Each inflow arrives, contributes to capacity, and then passes, replaced by the next. The system is therefore not built on what income is at any single point, but on how it behaves as it continues. The continuity of that movement is what allows the system to function. When income is understood as flow, stability is no longer tied to accumulation, but to the persistence of that flow across time.

This movement does not occur in a stable or uniform environment. Variability is inherent. Inflows differ in magnitude, arrive at different intervals, and respond to changing conditions. Interruption is not an anomaly but an expected condition within the system. There are periods where inflow is reduced, delayed, or absent. These disruptions do not exist outside the system; they are part of its normal operation. The system is therefore not defined by the absence of disruption, but by its ability to continue functioning through it.

The presence of variability and interruption introduces uncertainty into the flow. The system cannot assume that each future inflow will match the last in timing or magnitude. It must operate with incomplete continuity, where gaps and deviations occur. Stability, in this context, cannot mean the elimination of these conditions. It must instead mean the ability to sustain function while they occur. The system is tested not when flow is uninterrupted, but when it is not.

Structure determines how the system responds to these conditions. The arrangement of inflows, the distribution of dependency, and the organization of components define the system's capacity to absorb disruption. Structure is not visible in any single moment of flow, but it becomes apparent when that flow is stressed. It determines whether variability is absorbed or amplified, whether interruption is contained or propagated. The system inherits its behavior from this structure, responding according to how it has been configured rather than how it intends to operate.

Within this structure, liquidity acts as the mechanism that converts flow into continuity. As inflows arrive, they are not consumed instantaneously. A portion is retained, forming a buffer that allows the system to operate independently of exact inflow timing. This buffer bridges the gap between irregular inflows and continuous obligations. It absorbs deviations in timing and magnitude, allowing the system to maintain function even when flow is imperfect. Liquidity does not eliminate variability; it translates it into a form the system can sustain.

The presence of liquidity creates runway. Runway is the expression of capacity in time. It measures how long the system can continue to operate without additional inflow. This duration is not fixed; it expands when liquidity is preserved and contracts when it is depleted. Runway defines the temporal boundary within which the system can function under constraint. It represents the extension of flow beyond its immediate presence, allowing the system to persist through periods of interruption.

Time becomes the central dimension of stability. The system does not fail at the moment of disruption, but when its capacity to sustain function across time is exhausted. Runway determines whether interruptions can be absorbed or whether they lead to breakdown. The length of this runway reflects the system's ability to convert past inflow into future continuity. It is through this conversion that the system maintains operation across uneven conditions.

From this time capacity emerges decision space. Decision space is the range of actions that can be taken without compromising continuity. It is not defined by theoretical possibilities, but by what the system can sustain given its available time and capacity. When runway is extended, decision space expands. The system can delay action, evaluate alternatives, and adjust its course without immediate consequence. When runway is compressed, decision space contracts. The system must act quickly, often within a narrow set of viable options.

This relationship between time and decision space defines how the system behaves under pressure. As runway shortens, the system's ability to choose among alternatives diminishes. Decisions become constrained by immediacy, with priority given to maintaining function rather than optimizing outcomes. The quality of decisions reflects the conditions under which they are made. Limited time reduces the range of viable actions, shaping behavior through constraint rather than preference.

The interaction between flow, liquidity, runway, and decision space forms a continuous chain. Income enters as movement, is converted into stored capacity, extends into time, and manifests as optionality. Each stage transforms the previous one, linking the structure of income to the behavior of the system. Disruption at any point in this chain propagates through the rest. Variability affects liquidity, liquidity affects runway, runway affects decision space, and decision space influences the system's trajectory.

Within this chain, instability emerges as a compression of continuity. Variability that cannot be absorbed reduces liquidity. Reduced liquidity shortens runway. Shorter runway limits decision space. Limited decision space leads to constrained behavior, which can further destabilize the system. This compression does not occur as a single event, but as a process that unfolds across time. Each stage reinforces the next, narrowing the system's capacity to sustain itself.

Stability, by contrast, is the preservation of this chain. It is the condition in which flow continues to be converted into capacity, capacity into time, and time into optionality without breakdown. Stability does not require uniform inflow or the absence of disruption. It requires that the system maintain its ability to function despite these conditions. The continuity of flow is not defined by perfection, but by persistence.

This persistence depends on the system's ability to absorb variability without exhausting its capacity. When inflows fluctuate, the system must adjust without depleting liquidity beyond recovery. When interruptions occur, it must sustain operation long enough for flow to resume or be replaced. The system's structure determines whether these adjustments can be made without collapse. Stability is therefore not a fixed state, but a dynamic condition maintained through continuous adaptation.

The system does not operate in isolation from constraint. Capacity is finite, adjustment is limited, and prior structure cannot be easily reconfigured. These constraints define the boundaries within which the system must maintain continuity. Stability is achieved not by eliminating these limits, but by operating effectively within them. The system must sustain function with the structure it has, absorbing disruption without exceeding its capacity to adapt.

As the system moves through time, its stability is continuously tested. Each instance of variability, each interruption, and each decision interacts with the structure that supports it. The outcome of these interactions determines whether continuity is preserved or degraded. The system does not reach a final state of stability; it maintains stability through ongoing function. The persistence of this function across changing conditions defines its durability.

When the system is viewed in its entirety, the individual components merge into a single model. Flow, variability, liquidity, runway, and decision space are not separate elements, but interconnected stages of the same process. Each stage reflects a transformation of the previous one, linking the behavior of income to the behavior of the system. The continuity of flow across these transformations defines whether the system remains stable.

Income stability, in this final form, is not a measure of income itself. It is the ability of the system to sustain its function across time despite variability, interruption, and constraint. It is the preservation of flow through structure, the conversion of that flow into time, and the maintenance of decision space within that time. Stability is the continuity of this process, where each stage supports the next without breakdown.

The system does not eliminate disruption. It incorporates it. Variability, gaps, and shocks are conditions the system must navigate, not conditions it can avoid. Stability is achieved when these conditions do not interrupt the system's ability to function. The system continues, not because it is free from disruption, but because it is structured to sustain itself through it.

In this way, the continuity of flow becomes the defining characteristic of stability. It is the thread that connects each component of the system, from the arrival of income to the execution of decisions. When this thread is maintained, the system persists. When it is broken, the system degrades. Stability is therefore not a state to be reached, but a process to be sustained.

Income stability is the continuity of flow across time under constraint, where the system maintains its function by converting inflow into capacity, capacity into duration, and duration into viable choice.

This continuity does not exist as a fixed state, nor does it persist without effort. It must be maintained through the ongoing interaction of flow, structure, and constraint. Each period of operation either reinforces or weakens the system's ability to sustain itself, depending on how effectively it preserves capacity and absorbs disruption. Stability is therefore not something the system achieves once, but something it continually produces through its behavior across time.

The system continues only as long as this process holds. When flow can be converted into capacity, extended into time, and translated into viable action, continuity is preserved. When this process breaks at any stage, the system contracts, and its ability to sustain itself diminishes. The difference between stability and instability is not the presence or absence of disruption, but whether the system can continue to operate through it without losing function.

In this sense, income stability is not defined by what the system has, but by what it can continue to do. It is the persistence of function under constraint, the ability to sustain movement through time despite variability, and the maintenance of continuity across changing conditions. The system endures not by avoiding disruption, but by remaining intact as it passes through it.

About the Author

Mark Ellison writes about structural durability in systems exposed to volatility.

His work focuses on long-horizon stability across financial architecture, career positioning, cognitive resilience, and physical capacity. Rather than treating these domains as separate disciplines, he approaches them as interdependent systems governed by load, margin, buffer depth, and threshold behavior.

The Stability framework examines how fragility accumulates gradually and how disciplined structural calibration preserves optionality across decades. The objective is not optimization for peak outcomes, but preservation of functional continuity under variance.

Money Stability is part of a broader multi-domain stability ecosystem developed under Perennial Publishing, each domain addressing a distinct vector of long-term durability.

The work is designed for readers who prefer structural clarity over motivational rhetoric and long-horizon coherence over short-term intensity.

The Money Stability Series

Money Stability: *How to Build Financial Control in an Unstable World* (Cornerstone Volume)

Liquidity and Runway: *How to Build Financial Time, Extend Your Runway, and Stay Stable in an Unstable Economy*

Income Stability: *How to Build Predictable, Durable, and Resilient Income*

Future Titles include:

Expense Stability

Part of a Broader Stability Framework

The Money Stability Series is part of a larger stability ecosystem published by Perennial Publishing.

Related domains include:

Metabolic Stability — biological load, energy, and recovery capacity

Career Stability — income durability, positioning, and transition resilience

Mental Stability — cognitive steadiness under pressure and uncertainty

Emotional Stability — regulatory steadiness in environments that do not slow down

Each domain approaches stability as a structural problem: capacity versus load, buffers versus shocks, and governance versus drift. Together, they form a unified framework for long-horizon durability across the major systems that determine life trajectory.

About Perennial Publishing

Perennial Publishing produces practical systems guides for building stability in an unstable world.

Our books explore the foundations of long-term resilience across health, finance, career, and everyday decision-making. Each title focuses on clear frameworks, durable principles, and practical strategies that help readers build lasting stability rather than short-term fixes.

The Perennial catalog includes series on metabolic health, financial stability, career systems, and personal consistency. While each book stands on its own, they share a common goal: helping individuals create durable systems that support a stable and sustainable life.

For bulk or institutional orders, contact Perennial Publishing.

Made in United States
North Haven, CT
04 November 2026

21765028R00106